I0705411

SHIVERING

Heating Up

~~Cooling Down~~

THE GLOBAL WARMING DEBATE

RICHARD E. KLEIN, PhD

DUMB
DICKIE
PRESS.

Published by Dumb Dickie Press

ISBN-13: 979-8-6650-4498-9

The Dumb Dickie Press logo is a trademark of Richard E. Klein.

Cover design by Ellen Meyer and Vicki Lesage

TABLE OF CONTENTS

INTRODUCTION

"Even brave men shiver."
~ George R.R. Martin

What is the Climate Change Question?

IN THE FIRST EDITION OF *SHIVERING*, I addressed the topic of climate change and shared my revolutionary new hypothesis about glaciation causation. Following its initial publication in 2020, additional insights have arisen [1]. After receiving both positive and negative feedback, I realized I needed to write an updated second edition at a higher technical level. Readers familiar with physics, chemistry, and mathematics at the calculus level will get more out of this updated version.

The conjectures put forth in the 2020 edition of *Shivering* have now been revised. I do not claim that any of them have been validated. Instead, I preface many statements by "it is conjectured that…"

Unravelling the mysteries surrounding the Earth's climate isn't easily put into a 30-second sound bite. I have strived to use language that is understandable to a lay reader but in some areas had to dive into more technical details to substantiate my claims.

Two baffling questions face mankind about the Earth's climate:

- What caused the Earth's periodic ice ages, also referred to as glaciations?

- Is climate change being impacted by the presence of mankind?

The second question can only be answered after resolving the first. Attempting to answer the global warming question without consideration of ice age causation is akin to rearranging the deck chairs on the Titanic. Vessels at sea don't have billiards tables in the lounge, as a game of billiards is pointless when the billiard table is being tossed about. Analogously, arguing the merits of climate change and its causes is pointless if the climate is experiencing violent rises and drops. Addressing the periodic ice age causation question therefore takes precedence.

Answering climate change questions is a formidable feat. When viewed as an orchestration of many simultaneous events, the identification of a sole driving mechanism is elusive. The problem is complex in nature, and our available arsenal of tools is seemingly inadequate.

The mechanics of Earth's radiation balance are indeed complex. Tens of thousands of mechanisms are simultaneously impacting Earth's temperature. We also know that Earth's climate record, revealed to us based on sedimentary deposits and ice core drillings, exhibits rhythmical dynamics. The occurrence of rhythmic behavior even in a high order system strongly suggests that a small number of dynamic mechanisms are in command. The challenge is in identifying which of the many candidate mechanisms is responsible for setting the rhythm.

Because consensus has been hard to come by, climatologists have been quick to name sundry culprits. I am reminded of the line in the 1943 movie *Casablanca,* where Police Captain Renault issues the command, "Round up the usual suspects." There are many possible suspects, so those attempting to answer the climate causation question are stuck in a seeming quandary.

As one pursues an answer, it's best to focus on seeking the elephant in the room. Although the culprit, or mechanism, is yet to be identified, the inevitability of a primary culprit being there shouts out.

Of course, my sinister side has already hatched a plan. As the only person in the world who realizes that the world's climate is controlled by events local to the Earth, I can use that knowledge to hold the Earth's inhabitants hostage by claiming control. People worldwide would have to pay me a handsome ransom to prevent me from going out secretly at night and changing the Earth's ambient temperature. I can threaten to melt the ice caps or make Hawaii so cold that their tourist trade dwindles to a trickle. Among other fiendish schemes, I could go out in my secret deep-water submarine and release tubes of Alka-Seltzer® tablets. The Alka-Seltzer tablets will cause the ocean to spawn bubbles that rise, thus changing the Earth's albedo.

My money problems will completely disappear. I'll sell ocean flood insurance to all the nervous residents of Miami and Martha's Vineyard. I'll collect premiums but never have to pay out claims as I alone know that another ice age is coming. With the profits from my insurance scam, I'll buy up beachfront properties worldwide. I'll get the world's finest resorts for mere pennies on the dollar. After I get bored with that, I can release my butterflies along the Amazon River. The flapping of their little wings will spawn hurricanes galore. New Orleans will be forced to cancel Mardi Gras festivities. I would have the world at my mercy. Ha-ha-ha, what fun I could have while getting rich!

But alas, as a realist and a good guy, I accept that I will never be able to prove my hypothesis. On the other hand, it's nearly impossible for anyone else to prove me wrong, as it's unlikely we'll still be around to debate this 90,000 years from now, when I estimate the next glacial maxima will occur.

I am at a position in my life where I can sit back, reflect, throw out a few remarks, and let the cadre of young energetic zealots write grant proposals, pump out papers that few will ever read, and presumably get tenure within academia.

I've pondered the nuances associated with Earth's climate dynamics for the past half century. The Earth's climate machinery is complex, to say the least. My arguments are embedded in a level of mathematics that few have had the time or inclination to study. I have paid my club membership dues. I consider myself qualified to discuss the Earth's heat balance and thus climate dynamics, especially when viewed as a dynamic system. Skepticism is foundational to science and so I invite my critics to show me where my facts, reasoning, and/or conclusions are flawed. Until then, please enjoy with an open mind.

Read on to learn how the Earth is presently shivering, the underlying principles of my Kleinian Glacial Causation Hypothesis, and what's in store for our planet in the next 90,000 years and beyond. Grab a coat and scarf… we're about to dive into my ice age theory.

THE KLEINIAN GLACIAL CAUSATION HYPOTHESIS

The Glacial Causation Mystery

DETERMINING THE CAUSATION of the seemingly periodic glaciations and deglaciations has intrigued scientists as well as inquisitive lay people for several centuries.

My initial interest in the topic was spurred by a report of a Greenland ice core study published in the early 1970s. Following that, more findings related to climate records have appeared.

The evidence of global periodic ice ages on Earth is overwhelming and beyond question. This evidence comes in many forms, most notably geological, ice core sampling, and ocean floor sediment core samples. By boring into ocean seabeds and also into ice caps in various locations, researchers have reconstructed records of past climate conditions.

The data sources are complementary in location, precision, and timeline, each with strengths and weaknesses. Sediment core samples are available in a broad area and give low precision information about the climate over a range of many millions of years. The ice core samples are believed to provide reliable data about the climate for the last 800,000 years. Because these are extracted from ice, they are limited to the polar regions of the earth.

Evidence abounds that ice ages and periodic fluctuations in climate were indeed worldwide in scope. Strong correlations exist between samples taken over vast geographical areas. For example, Pacific and Caribbean seabed sediment cores jointly confirm the findings from ice core samples from both Greenland and Antarctica.

In short, there is universal agreement as to the past existence of worldwide periodic climate swings.

It's All About Dynamic Systems

MY THEORY RELIES HEAVILY on a concept embodied by two words: "dynamic systems." The word "dynamic" implies moving or changing. The word "systems" is harder to pin down, as it has many definitions. However, when "systems" is joined with the adjective "dynamic," it refers to a specific type of system. Here is a definition of a dynamic system:

*A collection or assembly of multiple components that
have or can possess time dependency.*

The dynamic system is governed by forces, torques, chemistry, heat principles, and other sundry physics. The dynamic system is subject to the laws of physics. And the laws of physics are inviolate.

In order to ultimately come to grips with the climate change question, one must first grasp the underlying mathematical relationships, and then be able to say something definitive. I assert that any attempt to understand climate change will fail if the role of feedback systems theoretic principles is left out. However, most people are not versed in feedback systems theory. The mathematical underpinnings of A. M. Lyapunov (1857-1918) are foundational to understanding climate change—and yet nearly all so-called climate science experts aren't informed on Lyapunov's stability concepts.

The standard approaches of science fall short. No simulation or computer model can capture the full dynamics. The order of the Earth's climate is too great. Its structure is unknown. No physical experiment can bring closure to this matter. It would be a waste of time to try. The climate change question therefore cannot be answered using the standard approaches.

An alternate approach is to examine Earth's climate record and attempt to infer the governing dynamics based on pattern recognition and reasoning. Let's get to it!

Working Toward a Hypothesis

As I mentioned, I became interested in glacial causation in the early 1970s. In 1971, I came upon an article that discussed a then-recent Greenland ice core that showed a temperature plot of the Earth's atmosphere going back sufficient years to provide one complete ice age cycle. I noted a distinct cycle, one that indicated a rapid recovery or reversal in temperature as the Earth rebounded robustly out of the most recent ice age. That ice age is commonly called the Wisconsin. In 1972, I published my first peer-reviewed paper on this topic [2].

The cycle resembled an inverted sawtooth. That one cycle had an abrupt character, with a jump in temperature around 12,000 YBP (years before present).

The combination of one complete cycle plus the abruptness at one distinct point within the cycle immediately attracted my attention. Please understand: I lived in a world of mathematics, closed-loop feedback systems, and electronic analogue computing. I knew what I was seeing, as I was familiar with the simulation of and theory behind such observed behaviors.

Upon observing this, I proceeded to formulate a candidate glacial causation hypothesis. Briefly stated, here is the underpinning of my hypothesis:

The Earth's climate record, as pertaining to the 100,000 year cycles during the recent Pleistocene, is conjectured to be the result of a self-regenerating mechanism, commonly known in systems theoretic terminology as a limit cycle.

The Vostok and Other Records

THE BIG PRIZE, in my view, came with the Vostok ice core record, published in 1985. The Vostok expedition involved the collective work of scientists from three nations—the Soviet Union, France, and the United States—at the Soviet station on the ice cap above Lake Vostok, a deeply submerged lake in Antarctica.

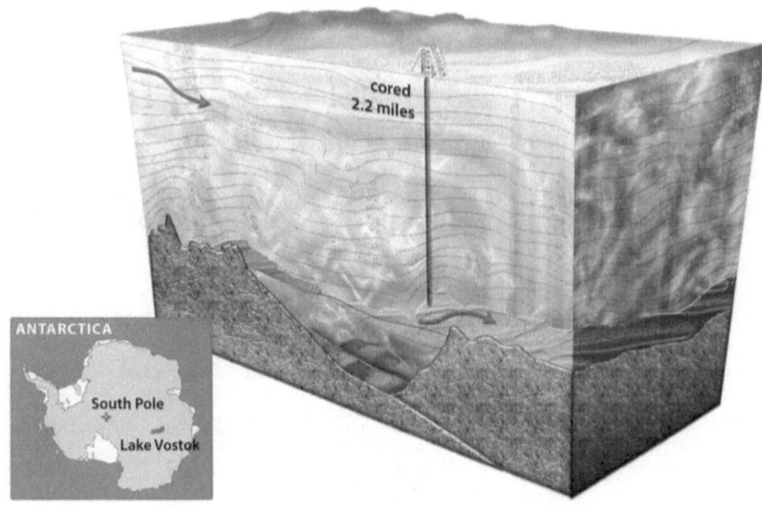

Depth of Lake Vostok Ice Core

The sketch above [3] illustrates the physical challenge of drilling and obtaining the Vostok ice core. The ice cap at that location was approximately 3,600 meters (or 2.2 miles) in thickness. The Vostok borings yielded a climate record that spanned 420,000 years of Earth temperature history. The Vostok record also yielded a host of other data, including various gas and particulate concentrations.

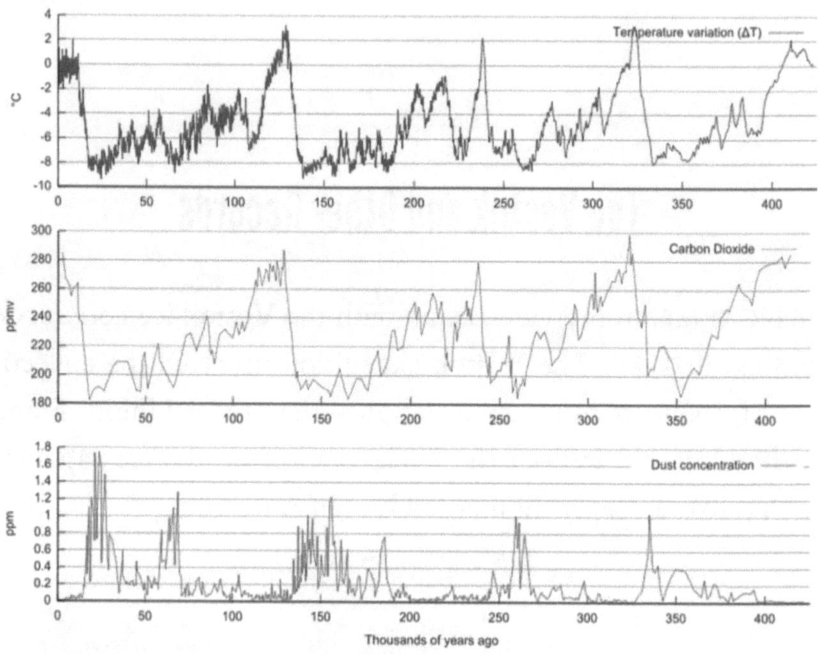

Vostok Ice Core Data

Note in this figure that time runs from right to left, so the most recent time period is to the left. The three variables shown, from top to bottom respectively, are temperature, atmospheric carbon dioxide concentration, and airborne dust or particulate concentrations.

The ice core contains a long, accurate record of the temperature at Vostok, as well as the atmospheric composition. The first graph shows the temperature record in terms of delta, or difference, from the current average world temperature, measured in degrees Celsius. For purposes of the graph, the current temperature is represented by 0. The middle graph shows the relative carbon dioxide in the atmosphere, measured in parts per million based on volume (ppmv). The lower graph represents the amount of particulate matter in the atmosphere, measured in parts per million (ppm).

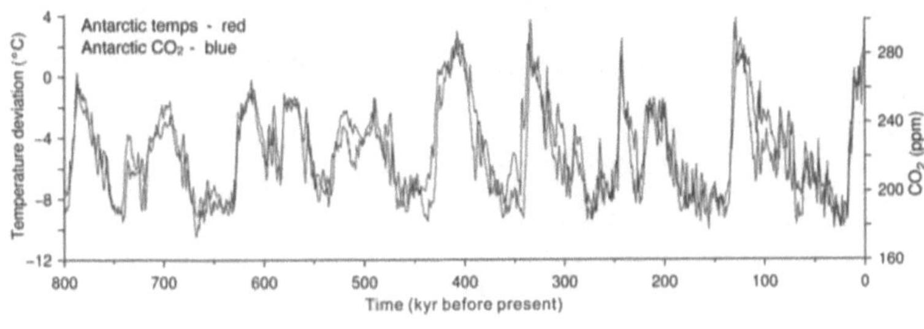

EPICA Ice Core Data

About a decade after Vostok, in 1996, a group of European countries reported on another such ice core drilling in Antarctica. This project was referred to as the EPICA (European Project for Ice Coring in Antarctica) ice core drilling. The EPICA ice core went back 800,000 years rather than 420,000. The findings from both of these ice cores agreed during the last 420,000 years, but EPICA added new data in that it confirmed the existence of more cyclical ice ages [4].

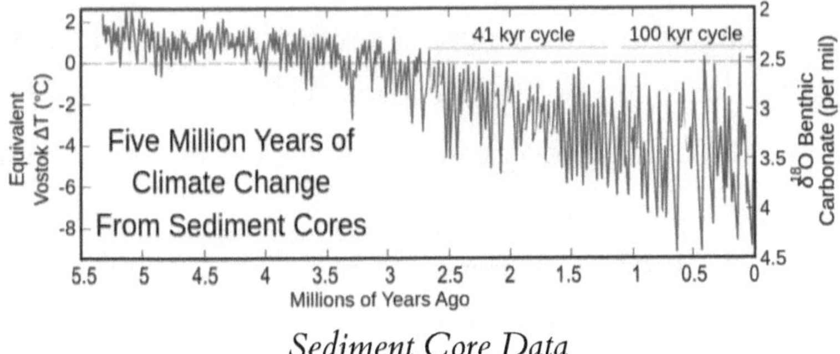

Sediment Core Data

Sediment core sampling [5], shown in this figure, confirms the Vostok ice core record by showing the correlation of temperature deltas derived from the sediment core to those determined by the Vostok ice core, while also extending considerably deeper back in time. This sediment core record, actually a record compiled from a combination of over 50 core samples across the globe, proclaims a strong message regarding Earth's climate over the last 5.5 million years. The researchers who prepared this figure opted to depict time running from left to right.

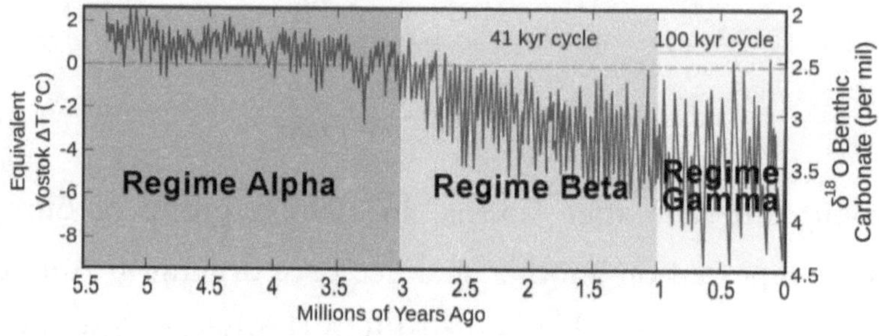

Earth Temperature History Regimes

Three distinct regimes are evident in the sediment core figure. These three regimes are vital to my explanation of ice age causation. Bear in mind that I am trained as a systems theorist, a person adept at examining dynamic fluctuations. My expertise is in inferring the mathematical models and systems that generated such records. I am akin to a doctor with a stethoscope—listening to a heartbeat and diagnosing the condition of the patient. This isn't my first rodeo.

As I continue in my diagnosis of Patient Earth, I will repeatedly refer to these three regimes:

• **REGIME ALPHA.** For the period from 5.5 million YBP to about three million YBP, the climate remained closely within a restricted temperature band. The temperature variations were of shorter periods, compared to more recent climate history. Temperatures on average were warmer than the present interglacial era. Presumably, less ice was present as permanent ice caps and snow cover. Ocean levels were higher due to a lesser volume of stored ice resting on land masses.

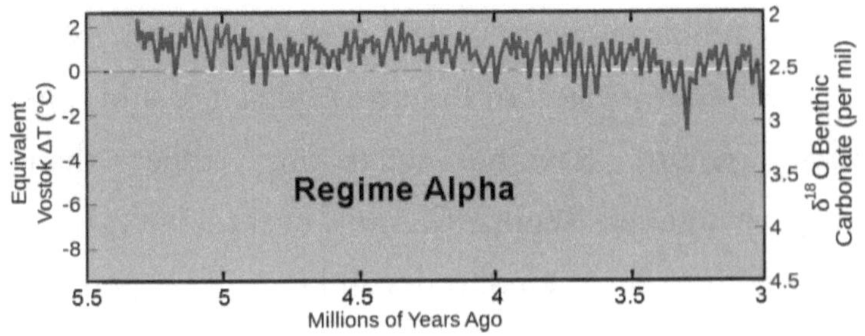

Regime Alpha Temperature Cycles

• **REGIME BETA.** Next, in the middle range of time spanning from three million YBP to one million YBP, the record transitioned to one dominated by a cycle of temperature swings with a predominant period of 41,000 years. To my modestly trained eye as a systems theorist, I feel that the 41K year cycles in Regime Beta tended to grow somewhat in amplitude, or size of oscillation, with the passage of time. This suggests that the stability of the 41K year cycles in this time period is an unresolved question. Also, a cooling trend, on average for this period, was evident. Ice caps started to increase in mass, albeit slowly. Likewise, ocean levels started a slow descent. Clearly, the presence of the observed 41K year cycles coincides with the obliquity periods as studied by Milankovitch [6]. Because of the correlation of the 41K year cycles with the obliquity periodicity, proponents of the Milankovitch cycles accept the coincidence as causal proof. This may well be the case, however, other unsolved questions arise. If the 41K year cycles caused such strong swings in Regime Beta, why are similar temperature swings not evident in Regime Alpha and Regime Gamma? If the Milankovitch obliquity cycle argument holds in Regime Beta, the same physics must also be at work both before and after Regime Beta. Not only are Regime Alpha and Regime Gamma devoid of any visible evidence of 41K year cycles, entirely different behaviors were taking place. In Regime Alpha, it would appear that the climate record was non-fluctuating, other than slow temperature changes. In Regime Gamma, cyclical fluctuations were present, but with stronger amplitudes and far greater periods, about 100K years in periodicity.

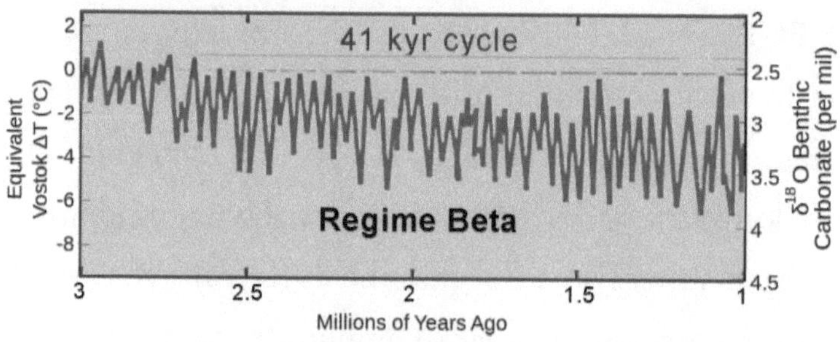

Regime Beta Temperature Cycles

• **REGIME GAMMA.** In the third and most recent period, from one million YBP up until the present era, a strong cycle with a 100,000 year period dominated. The 100K year cycles clearly exhibited greater bottom-to-peak amplitudes in swing compared to the 41K year cycles present before one million years ago.

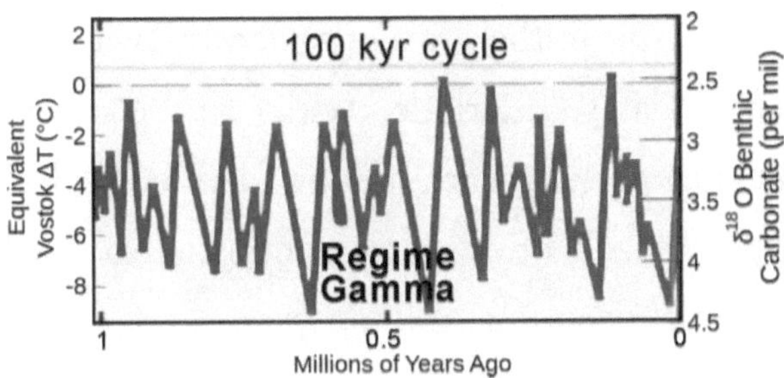

Regime Gamma Temperature Cycles

I will leave the matter of the stability of the 100K year cycle as yet another open question. The bottom point of each cycle is approximately uniform. The downward moving average appears to have halted or lessened. It's as if the cycles bottomed out at some type of barrier or hard stop. I use the word average to refer to an average based on a moving window of time, where the moving window's duration is equal to the period of the base cycle, i.e. 100,000 years. The volume of ice continued to increase in the polar regions and also on land masses as glaciers and permanent snow and ice coverage.

The above discussion does not take into account any potentially longer period that might be associated with the general downward temperature trend. The sediment core figure, in and of itself, with its general downward trend in temperature over 5.5 million years is insufficient to permit one to conclude whether or not any longer (lower frequency) oscillation in temperature exists.

Another observation is that the Earth's average temperature (again, referring to a 100K year moving window average) over the most recent one million years was significantly colder compared to the brief interglacial or warm period in which mankind now lives. Said another way, during the most recent one million years of

Earth's climate, being in the grips of an ice age was more the norm by far than today's interlude with its relatively moderate temperatures. The present warm period, defined as the most recent 12,000 years, is indeed brief when contrasted to the longer time period of the most recent one million years.

In thinking of these three Regimes, I am reminded of the fable from India regarding a group of blind men who encounter a large animal called an elephant. The blind men, being adept at touch, decide to feel the elephant in order to know more about it. One man touches the side of the elephant, remarking that it is like a wall. A second man touches a leg, saying that the elephant is like a pillar, much akin to a tree trunk. A third man touches the ear and says the elephant is like a large fan. A fourth man touches the elephant's trunk saying it is like a large snake. Yet another man touches the elephant's tusk saying it is hard and smooth like a spear. Lastly, a blind man touches the tail saying it is like a rope.

The record of Earth's climate for the last 5.5 million years bears analogy to the elephant. In each of the three Regimes as defined, Earth's climate record has its own unique characteristics. In Regime Alpha, one sees a slowly changing time variation with slight short characteristic variations. Little is happening as the Earth slowly drifts towards a cooler climate.

In Regime Beta, one sees a steady decline accompanied by cyclical variations of a 41K year periodicity. In this regime, the climate record seems to be reacting to external drivers, both over the entirety of Regime Beta as the mean temperature drops and as the 41K year cyclical variations appear.

Quite in contrast, in Regime Gamma the 100K year cyclical

variation is dominant. Moreover, the variation repeats itself having a sawtooth characteristic, accompanied by a hard bottom and an abrupt rebound, although in staggered steps. For Regime Gamma, the time history exhibits a behavior akin to a self-generated cycle.

Although each of the three regimes has its own respective behavior, one must arguably conclude that each must be compatible with the others. Like the elephant and the blind men, in order to grasp the entirety of the climate record, it is incumbent on us to see how the three regimes can coexist and thus behave as an elephant—a unified climate record.

The Mix of Chaotic Behavior and Regularity

IN THIS DISCUSSION, I refer to the most recent 5.5 million years of Earth's climate record. During this time, the Earth's climate machine—yes, it can be considered a machine—exhibited both fluid and yet ordered behaviors.

It was fluid in the sense that, like weather, it was chaotic and possibly even random. Another word describing this behavior is stochastic.

But there is also a certain degree of order and regularity shown in the climate record. I believe that the long-term climate dynamic mechanisms were strongly ordered, as evidenced by the presence of the distinctive 100K year inverted sawtooth waveform in Regime Gamma. I will refer later to the strong implications of this sawtooth waveform, which will play a central role as I discuss the ice age causation question pertaining to the prior one million years, Regime Gamma.

Because order was obviously present, it follows that we should be able to find an explanation for the order. The strong 100K year periodicity has a rhythm. I am inclined to think that a simple pattern should be caused by a simple mechanism. In contrast, if the mechanism was causally complex, then the simple structure or response would be more chaotic. Statisticians use the phrase "Monte Carlo" to denote behaviors of outcomes based on random occurrences of many independent events. Clearly, the observed 100K year cycles would not be the outcomes if Monte Carlo rules applied. The responsible mechanism must be, comparatively speaking, simple. My task as a sleuth is to identify that causation mechanism.

As a feedback systems theorist, I have now established the plausibility of a governing mechanism. Because the 100K year periodicity is so regular, I also know that the causation mechanism is simple, not complex or chaotic. Things that have simple rhythms tend to have simple explanations.

The Kleinian Glacial Causation Hypothesis

NOW THAT WE'VE DISCUSSED the importance of dynamic systems, along with the Vostok and other ice core records, we are almost ready to dive into my hypothesis. But first, a disclaimer concerning sequential versus simultaneous.

Limit cycles involve the outcomes of many simultaneous relationships. In mathematical terms, the simultaneous evolution of one or more differential equations is involved. Explaining simultaneous events with equations allows for a more rigorous discussion but can be difficult for the lay reader to understand. I have opted to use language instead, which has the shortcoming of being inherently sequential in nature yet perhaps easier to follow.

The Kleinian Glacial Causation Hypothesis can now be stated:

• Ice sheets slowly form, most notably in the northern hemisphere, causing Earth's albedo, or reflectivity, to increase.

• As ice sheet coverage increases, temperatures drop, thereby contributing to more temperature drop. This is presumed to be a positive feedback mechanism.

• As the Earth continues in its temperature decline, ice sheets expand on land, and to a lesser degree, on open ocean surfaces.

• The warmer belt centered on the equator is more stubborn in its fight to ward off freezing.

• The growth of ice coverage is subject to limitations. Because the warmer belt maintains itself, Earth's temperature ceases to drop. Ice sheets primarily in the northern hemisphere reach their limits and terminate at some mid-latitude point.

• As ice sheets reach their maxima on land, ice sheet maxima on floating sheet ice are also reached. In general, ice sheets on land extend to lower latitudes compared to ice sheets that cover open ocean water. As a visualization, let's assume that ice sheets on land extend down to approximately 40 degrees in latitude, such as the latitude of New York or Beijing in the northern hemisphere and Melbourne or Buenos Aires in the southern hemisphere. Also assume that sea ice extends down, to a lesser extent, to approximately 50 degrees latitude, such as Vancouver or London in the northern hemisphere and Christchurch, New Zealand in the southern hemisphere.

• During the glacial maxima, the ice sheets, notably covering ocean areas, are stable and remain in place.

• It is during this period, of approximately 10K years to possibly 15K years, that ocean dynamics and currents are modified.

• Because land areas in higher latitudes are largely ice covered, the flow of rivers into the ocean diminishes.

• As a general rule, circulation patterns in oceans diminish.

• It is assumed (but not proven) that seawater currents are reduced.

• Because ocean currents, notably in the mixed layer, are diminished, the mixed layer undergoes a temperature inversion. (Note: Various citations exist, but the mixing layer is normally presumed to involve approximately the first 200 meters of depth.) The frozen ice layer chills the water in proximity to that layer. In contrast, water deeper within the mixing layer is protected from exposure to a cooling mechanism. Also, water tends to act as an insulating body, meaning that water serves as its own insulation.

• The temperature inversion in the mixed layer is responsible then for a density inversion.

• As with all bodies of water that acquire a density inversion, an overturning results. The time scale for the overturning is brief, especially when compared to the timescale required for the development of the density inversion.

• Because atmospheric CO_2 degassing is limited following the hypothesized overturning, it is my view that the overturning is limited to the mixing layer.

• As the ocean flips in its attempt to achieve stability, two things occur simultaneously: (i) sea ice is now in the proximity of warmer water from the overturning, and (ii) the upwelling causes wave reactions.

• Because the sea water under the sea ice causes waves, some fracturing of the sea ice occurs. As bodies of water overturn, the overturning also creates wave actions. Wave actions taking place in deep water are not violent. Instead the waves, in the form of swells, migrate in a radial fashion. Then, as the wave encounters shallower waters, the physics of waves causes wave amplitudes to increase. Recall that surfers catch their wave when it is almost imperceptible, then they paddle vigorously to catch the wave. As their wave approaches the shoreline, its amplitude increases. When sea ice is present, waves won't transform into breakers, but the lifting action of the swells remains strong. I argue that waves obey the laws of wave mechanics, even should sheet ice cover the ocean. I argue that the mechanical breakage of sea ice is greatest—and most concentrated— adjacent to landmass shorelines. This causes discrete and large sections of sea ice to break away.

• Portions, and large portions at that, of sea ice are free to drift away. That drifting inevitably accelerates melting as warmer waters are encountered. It is plausible that as larger sheets of ice encounter warmer waters, additional fracturing due to thermal stress occurs.

• Oceanic overturning can be regional as opposed to global, thus being responsible for discrete fractures in subsequent melting of ice sheets.

• It is argued that the observed stair-step rebounds out of the glacial maxima are explained by the discrete nature in which sea ice sheets break up.

• Once large portions of former sea ice melt, Earth's albedo is significantly reduced, thereby causing the abrupt rebound in Earth's temperature.

• Once melting on the ice sheets is initiated, Earth's albedo is reduced, thus permitting the planet to enter into an interglacial period.

• And thus the cycle of causality is complete.

SUPPORTING MY THEORY

*"The universe shivers with wonder in the depths
of the human."*
~ Brian Swimme

Background on Limit Cycles

I've mentioned limit cycles a few times now. The term "limit cycle" has a precise mathematical as well as physical meaning. Limit cycles exhibit self-sustained oscillations for some set of parameters.

For our purposes, we can think of them as the oscillations, or swings, that are generated from within a system, rather than being caused by an external force. If the system is perturbed slightly, it returns to the stable limit cycle.

Consider a pendulum wall clock. All physical systems that exhibit limit cycle behavior have some type of energy source. In the case of a pendulum clock, the energy source is either a wound-up spring or a hanging weight that will lower itself. Obviously, a pendulum clock will eventually stop if the owner fails to properly wind it. The clock sustains its swinging because the clock's designer built in an escapement. The purpose of the escapement is to add a tiny push to the pendulum at every swing.

Pendulum Wall Clock

The pendulum clock is capable of keeping time because the period of swing of the pendulum is fixed. When a pendulum clock is in operation, it tells time reliably because the physics of the swinging pendulum dictate precision in periodicity.

In the study of dynamics and dynamic systems, the two major types of systems are linear systems and nonlinear systems (which is anything that's not linear). Limit cycles can only occur in nonlinear systems.

Because I suspected that cyclical glaciations were the result of limit cycles, I understood that I had to consider only nonlinear systems.

The adjectives linear and nonlinear have their origins in the language of lines. A straight line, with no curves and thus an infinite radius, is defined as having linear properties. Said another way, any relationship between two variables that is linear can be described by using a straight line. In contrast, any relationships that involve lines other than straight lines are called nonlinear, which includes curved lines and lines with discrete breaks and jumps.

Aerodynamic drag is an example of a nonlinear relationship. The aerodynamic drag acting on an object is proportional to the velocity squared, thus described by a parabolic curve and not a straight line. The dependent variable does not change in direct proportion to a change in any of the inputs.

If we consider Earth's temperature system and its radiation heat balance, numerous nonlinearities are present. One nonlinearity is that radiation is proportional to absolute temperature to the 4th power. Another example of a nonlinearity in the Earth's climate system is associated with how dramatically H_2O—that is, water— can change its properties as temperature varies. When water freezes, the reflectivity of ice changes abruptly and dramatically. H_2O in liquid form has a low albedo, typically about 0.1. In contrast, once water freezes and becomes ice, the albedo jumps dramatically, with 0.9 being typical. In short, Earth's climate system is highly nonlinear.

I will lighten up the discussion with a joke. A drunk is out at night searching underneath a streetlight.

A passerby asks the drunk, "What are you looking for?"

"A coin that I dropped," the drunk replies.

"Where did you drop the coin?"

"Down the street," the drunk says.

"Why are you looking here when you know the coin is elsewhere?" the passerby asks.

"Because this is where the light is."

We tend to look for answers in places where we have light, and that's why we look for answers using linear systems theory. We don't get many answers concerning nonlinear systems because we have very little light there.

The presence of nonlinearities in a system is a profound game changer. Limit cycles will sometimes appear within closed-loop dynamic systems. For the closed-loop system to be a candidate, it must contain nonlinearities.

"Hunting" is yet another descriptive term with the same limit cycle implications. Hunting commonly arises in closed-loop systems, especially those that also contain gear drives. In mechanical engineering, backlash is the lost motion in a mechanism caused by gaps between the parts.

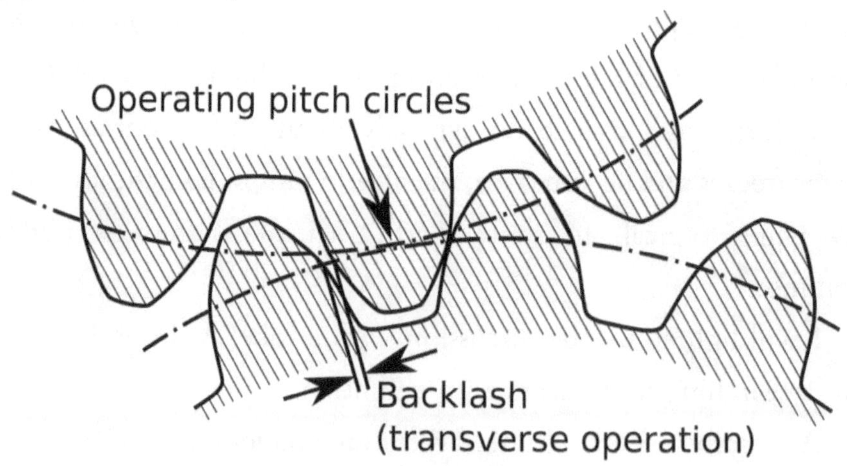

Gear Backlash [7]

An example is the amount of clearance between mated gear teeth in gear trains. It can be seen when the direction of movement is reversed and the slack or lost motion is taken up before the reversal of motion is complete. When tuning to minimize backlash, one result can be that the system continuously overshoots and then undershoots. This is often referred to as hunting. The closed-loop system with gear backlash will commonly exhibit oscillations of a specific periodicity and amplitude.

For those not well versed in limit cycles, I will elaborate.

I became familiar with limit cycles from my graduate level courses in systems and controls, including nonlinear systems dynamics.

Limit cycles are often associated with the work of the Russian mathematician A. M. Lyapunov.

A.M. Lyapunov

Lyapunov (1857-1918) studied stability of differential equation systems, nonlinear systems in particular. Lyapunov's Second or Direct Method, as well as Lyapunov V-Functions, applies to nonlinear systems.

I could expound on the mathematical underpinnings of Lyapunov's work and limit cycles in nonlinear feedback systems, but instead I'll discuss limit cycles that appear in everyday life.

The Old Faithful geyser in Yellowstone National Park is an illustration of a limit cycle. Old Faithful erupts with regularity every 65 minutes, give or take ten minutes.

Old Faithful

The eruption occurs because of internal dynamics. It has nothing to do with anything astronomical. Following each eruption and subsequent vacating of the underground vertical vents, ground water seeps in and refills the geyser's emptied subterranean vents.

Heat from the Earth's mantle in turn raises the water's temperature until the water eventually boils, producing steam. The steam pressure forces the standing column of water upward in a sudden rush. As the vertical vent empties, its hydrostatic pressure at lower depths lessens. The process then starts over, thus repeating itself. As with all limit cycles, the amplitude and periodicity result from the loop dynamics—not due to any outside force.

Shivering occurs when humans or other warm-bodied creatures become chilled. It's the result of internal, involuntary actions. People cannot make themselves shiver. When shivering takes place, it adopts a cyclical timing. As a self-induced phenomenon, it is aptly described as a limit cycle. The dynamics are internal to and regulated by the shivering body.

There are many limit cycles that occur in nature and around us. Percolation of coffee is a limit cycle. Certain predator-prey populations will exhibit cyclical behavior over time. A jackhammer that runs on compressed air functions, by design, as a limit cycle.

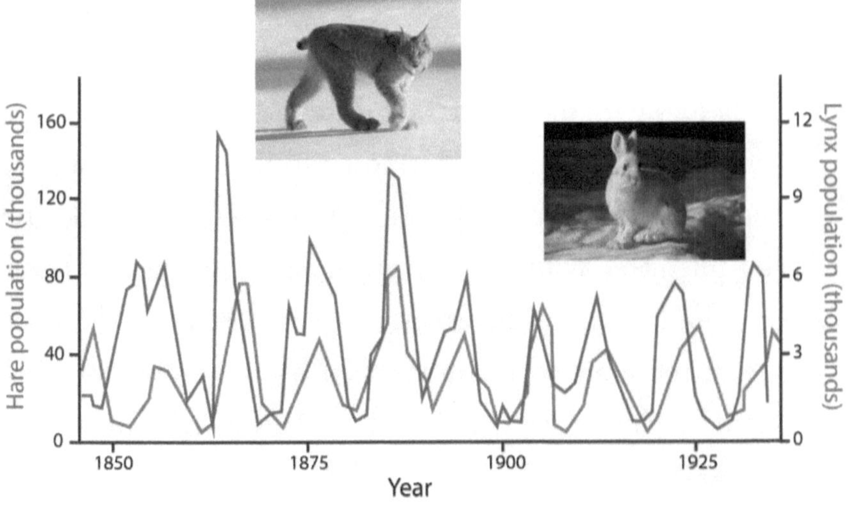

Predator-Prey Population Model Dynamics [8]

Even the phrase "squeaky clean" owes its origin to limit cycles as the squeaking sound generated by rubbing one's finger over a clean dish or window is cyclical in nature. The sound emanates because the rubbing of the finger initiates a start and stop friction mechanism. Static friction and dynamic friction have two different values, called coefficients of friction. Once sliding initiates, the coefficient of friction lessens. Upon cessation of sliding, the static or Coulomb friction coefficient increases.

The farm implement that wobbles side-to-side as it's pulled down a road behind a vehicle typically wobbles because of limit cycle dynamics. The implement's side-to-side oscillation is usually due to backlash, as the implement's tongue has slop or excessive wear. This backlash, a form of nonlinearity, combines with the dry friction of the steel components rubbing on steel. In the case of a towed farm implement, the frequency of the oscillation will usually increase as the speed increases.

The screech of chalk or fingernails on a slate board is yet another limit cycle. Chatter in a machine tool cutting metal is due to a limit cycle.

Most homes with thermostats regulate the heating with a series of on/off commands from the thermostat to the furnace. Although the occupant doesn't necessarily notice, the household's temperature cyclically fluctuates within a narrow temperature band, thereby causing a limit cycle. The frequency, amplitude, and general character of the limit cycle are dictated by the properties of the house, furnace, duct system, and the hysteresis switch limits within the thermostat.

In short, examples of limit cycles abound all around us.

Limit cycles, wherever and whenever they occur, obey certain behavioral rules:

• If stable, the limit cycle will tend to assume a specific amplitude.

• Again, if stable, the limit cycle will oscillate at a given periodicity.

• Provided that the limit cycle is stable in the sense of Lyapunov, both the amplitude and periodicity are properties of the closed-loop dynamics.

• In systems with unstable limit cycles, other rules apply and the topic is complex. The climate record available to us is insufficient for determining unstable limit cycles.

• Some closed loop systems have nested, hence multiple, limit cycles. The trajectory, as it is called, can jump from one stable limit cycle to one of the nested cycles. This jumping can explain why observed oscillations can change in both period and amplitude.

Nonlinear systems with limit cycles exhibit several interesting properties not seen in the linear counterparts. Both the amplitude and the period of the limit cycle are predetermined. In a linear system such as a swinging pendulum, if you deflect the pendulum, assuming small angles, and then release it, the resulting amplitude of the swing is dependent upon how far you initially offset the pendulum. In a limit cycle dominated system, that's not the case. The amplitude when the trajectory has settled onto the limit cycle is a fixed property and is not influenced by the initial offset or perturbation.

I could discuss numerous other properties of limit cycles, but I suspect the reader might be near their limit. We've covered the most essential points and are ready to move on to the Vostok record.

Examining the Vostok Record

YOU DON'T HAVE TO BE A CLIMATE SCIENTIST to, upon examination of the 420,000 years of the Vostok record, recognize the distinct presence of the 100K year base cycle, and also its characteristic choppy or sawtooth waveform. The graphs are presented again below.

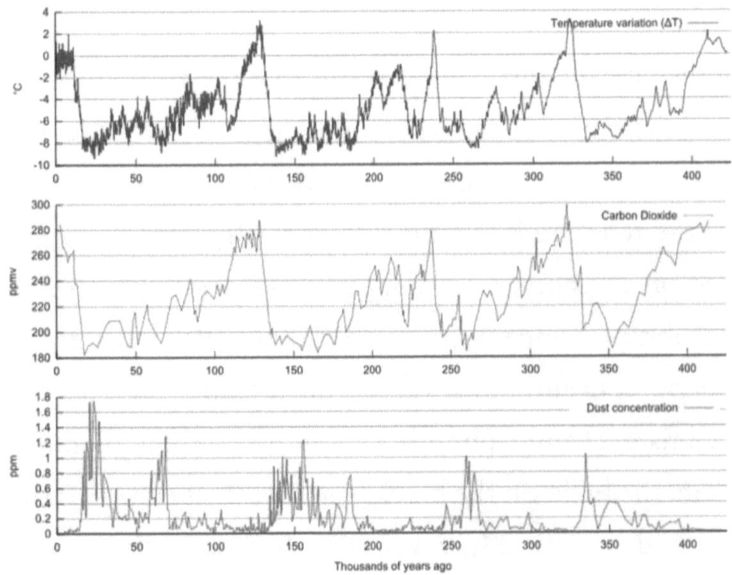

Vostok Ice Core Data

Another fact is evident: The three records—temperature, carbon dioxide, and particulates—are repetitious relative to each other. The same general trends were common within each cyclic 100K year period.

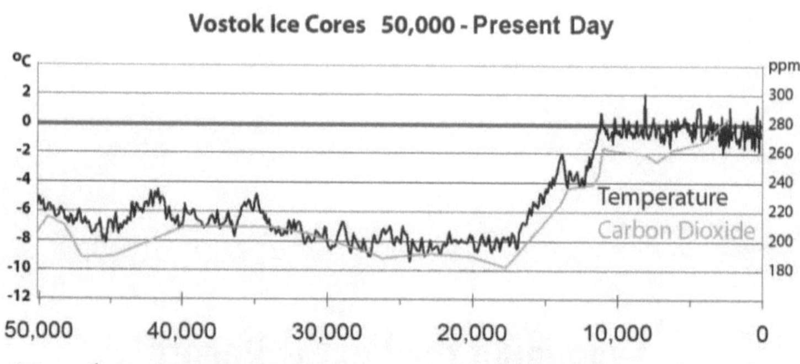

Vostok Ice Core Temperature and Carbon Dioxide Graph

This record of temperature and carbon dioxide for the past 50,000 years illustrates the abrupt rise in the Earth's climate. When the Earth last came out of an ice age, it came out with gusto. The abruptness of the periodic rebound in each cycle is of paramount significance.

Another fascinating observation is that the atmospheric carbon dioxide concentration lagged behind the temperature rebound. Findings suggest that the lag in carbon dioxide behind the temperature rebound is around 800 years [9].

Based on causality, a seeming paradox is squarely confronting us. The abrupt temperature rise 12,000 YBP leads the rise in atmospheric concentrations of carbon dioxide, not the converse. Many climate change pundits claim that carbon dioxide is the archvillain, the bully on the block, and that temperature is the meek follower and victim. However, the Vostok record makes this concern outright suspect. Note that this figure has been shown with time running from left to right.

The figure below shows other examples of carbon dioxide increase lagging behind the temperature rise between 270K and 350K YBP. There is a consistent record of this relationship, which tends to discredit the theory that carbon emissions are responsible for global warming.

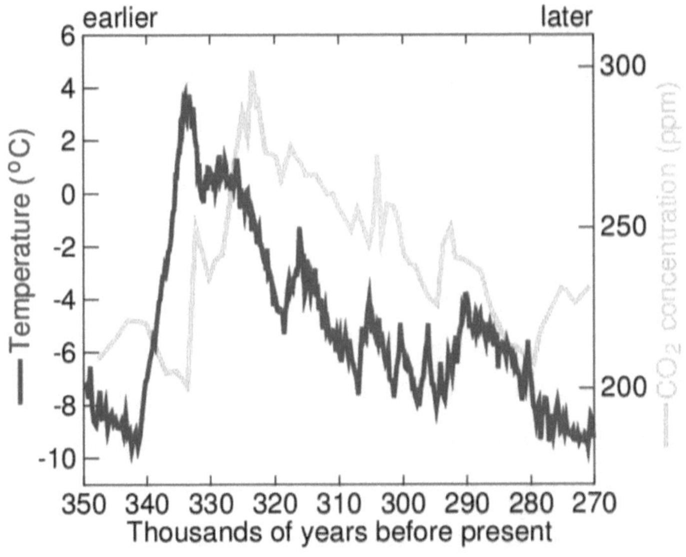

A Closer Look at the CO2 Lag

The evidence in the climate record of the existence of periodic glaciations is clear and compelling. The evidence of periodic ice ages and warmer interglacial periods is beyond debate. The why behind these records, however, is not obvious. A few questions jump out but remain unanswered:

1. What caused the glaciations? What mechanism is responsible for Earth to cool, thus sending it into each successive ice age?

2. What explains the approximate 100K year periodicity of the

glaciations in the last one million years? And why just in the last one million years?

3. What caused the 41K year periodic temperature swings starting about three million YBP, but were seemingly absent before then?

4. Why did the periodic fluctuations change from 41K year cycles to 100K year cycles about one million years ago?

5. Why did the amplitudes of these cycles increase at the time of the transition one million YBP?

6. In the most recent million years, what was responsible for the abruptness of the rebound out of each glacial period?

7. What mechanism explains why the rebound occurs in discrete steps?

8. Why do the glaciations over the most recent million years each bottom out at approximately the same lower bound?

9. What mechanism is behind the 21K year period oscillations superimposed on the 100K year sawtooth pattern in Regime Gamma?

10. If the Earth was in a general cooling trend over the period from 5.5 million YBP to one million YBP, what arrested that cooling trend?

Numerous explanations have been put forth, but none have come anywhere close to providing consistent and reasoned answers. Most proposed theories of glacial causation have been seriously discredited or lack substantiation.

Advances in ice core sampling, sea floor sediment testing, carbon dating, geology, astronomy, and isotope usage continue. Accordingly, those who study climate are benefiting from increases in the overall clarity, reliability, and certainty of the Earth's climate record. As such, whenever any new theory comes along or an older theory is dusted off and reexamined, it's becoming easier to scrutinize the theory to see if it conforms to the available data.

Because we have such a proliferation of data involving various parameters and time histories spanning the Vostok and EPICA record's timeframes, it's relatively straightforward to see if any theory passes muster. A candidate theory can be eliminated if it contradicts the existing data. On the other hand, validating a theory on climate is a Herculean undertaking. The existing tests are not conclusive; they only serve as relatively weak screening questions.

A Closer Examination of the Climate Record

THE KLEINIAN GLACIAL CAUSATION HYPOTHESIS rests heavily on the figure shown earlier of the Earth's temperature as reconstructed based on sediment cores. The time period spans from 5.5M YBP up until the relatively recent advent of mankind's modern civilization. By choice, I am not discussing yesterday's weather or if the ocean level is rising and thus putting Miami's streets under water. I am focusing on the most recent 5.5M years of Earth's climate record rather than debating what mankind is or isn't doing.

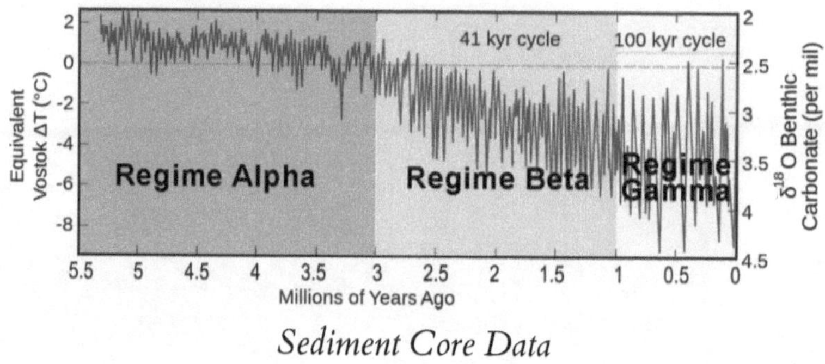

Sediment Core Data

Because of the graph's importance as I defend my hypothesis, I'm showing the figure again above.

As previously stated, I have divided the temperature record into three regimes:

I. Regime Alpha (5.5M YBP to 3M YBP)

II. Regime Beta (3M YBP to 1M YBP)

III. Regime Gamma (1M YBP to present)

As a believer in keeping things simple, I have accepted the temperature record as accurate. I have no grounds to question the validity of the record.

The Alpha Regime

I accept Regime Alpha as presented. I will not attempt to discuss its higher frequency fluctuations. During Regime Alpha, the record reflects a slow but steady cooling of the earth. I am reminded of the line by Big Jake, as played by John Wayne, "Your fault, my fault, nobody's fault, it won't matter" [10]. My point is simple: Knowing the reason for the temperature decline won't change much. Our focus is on trying to explain cyclical ice ages. Obviously, the Earth's cooling as evidenced in Regime Alpha aided the Earth in arriving at its later temperature, but the why doesn't contribute to answering the glacial causation mystery question.

Because Earth was warmer compared to present day (the era of mankind) averages, and because there were no significant glacial periods within Regime Alpha, there were relatively few ice formations. Glaciers, if any existed on the various land masses, had no appreciable ice volume. In other words, the Earth did not have any significant buildup of ice resting on land. Moreover, the oceans were also relatively free of icepack. This includes the Arctic Ocean.

Because of the relative absence of ice caps and glaciers on Earth, ocean levels were higher. Compared to present day sea levels, the oceans were possibly as much as 70 meters (about 230 feet) higher.

Because of the positioning of continental land masses around the Arctic Ocean, flow patterns were strongly influenced by the ocean level. During Regime Alpha, with its higher sea levels, the Arctic Ocean affected global weather since circulation patterns were less restricted.

Some mechanism was at work causing the gradual descent in Earth's temperature. Though knowing the precise cause makes little difference, my guess is that there were two main factors. The first and dominant factor was a gradual increase in Earth's albedo, as Antarctica acquired an ice and snow covering. A second but lesser mechanism was carbon dioxide removal from the atmosphere through ocean water absorption of carbon gases.

As Earth's temperature underwent a slow and gradual decline during Regime Alpha, this set the stage for (i) a drop in the moving average temperature of Earth, and (ii) the outbreak of the 41K year period oscillations to come in Regime Beta.

At this point, I've commented on events that occurred during the three distinct regimes of Earth's climate over the last 5.5M years. Let's recall that knowledge as we review the transitions between regimes—this is where we see how the oceans can, presumably, explain the climate record.

Alpha Regime Transitions to the Beta Regime

Two significant things happened leading up to the Alpha-to-

Beta transition, thereby causing the transition. First, Earth's temperature went into a slow and gradual decline. Second, the Arctic Ocean that had formerly been ice-free started to accumulate sea ice. The reduction in circulation along with the formation of quasi-permanent ice cover impacted the ability of the Arctic Ocean to dynamically drive worldwide weather patterns. These two factors then set the stage for the albedo, with its reinforcing positive feedback, to send the Earth into a condition where ice formation on both poles started to influence Earth's weather.

Regime Beta Experiences 41K Year Period Oscillations

In Regime Beta, the Earth experienced 41K year cycles. The Earth and its climate history hold their secrets well. I do not claim to have an answer but do have a conjecture. The scenario is weak and in great likelihood erroneous. So why am I presenting it? Well, we have only the sparsest of candidate explanations concerning the 41K periodicity in Regime Beta, so even if I'm later proved wrong, I hope the ingredients of my conjecture will become food for thought for others.

My conjecture requires that three things occur simultaneously: (i) the Earth is experiencing a mid-range in atmospheric temperature, thereby allowing albedo changes to occur because albedo is strongly influenced by the presence and absence of ice, (ii) the observed 41K periodicity coincides with the 41K periodicity in Earth's obliquity, and (iii) as the Earth's tilt or obliquity changes, by some process yet to be explained, the poles of the Earth shift in synchrony, and the pole locations cycle between oceans and landmasses.

This third ingredient—pole locations changing cyclically between land and sea—strongly impacts albedo. Because albedo can shift so dramatically and in a cyclical fashion, this in turn possibly explains the cyclical variations in Earth's temperature in Regime Beta. This phenomenon occurs only in Regime Beta as during Regime Alpha the earth is warm and thus relatively ice-free, and in Regime Gamma the poles are co-located in regions of permanent ice.

I start off with the working hypothesis that the 41K periodicity cycles are correlated to the 41K periodicity of Earth's obliquity, or tilt. Because Regime Alpha and Regime Gamma provide no hint of cyclical excitations at the 41K periodicity, I assume that Earth's thermal response to obliquity changes was weak to non-existent in regimes Alpha and Gamma.

Continental land masses in certain latitudes have more influence on albedo than others. For the sake of discussion, let's assume that land masses with such sensitivity to albedo are in higher latitude regions, from 55 degrees to 75 degrees latitude. Also, if we assume that the Earth's continents are configured as they are today, the major effects relate to the northern hemisphere.

So what mechanism caused Earth's albedo to become synchronized with Earth's obliquity? I conjecture that Earth's tilt somehow caused the north pole to change on Earth's spin axis relative to the planet's outer shell or surface. The location of the south pole may have changed relative to Antarctica, but that's not essential to the theory to be proposed.

Recall that the Earth has a molten core and that the shell, or mantle, is relatively thin. Earth's obliquity is defined relative to its orbital plane around the sun. What is not explained, at least to my satisfaction, is what happens to the planet as it varies in tilt. My proposed explanation of the 41K periodicity cycles within Regime Beta makes sense assuming that Earth's mantle shifts cyclically relative to the molten core. Thus, during the warmer portions of the 41K periodicity cycle, the north pole coincided with water and during colder portions of the cycle, the north pole coincided with continental land mass. So, in the warmer periods, the north pole experienced less ice coverage and thus a lower albedo. During the colder periods, the converse was true.

The next question is: Why did the 41K periodicity obliquity cycle act as a strong driver in Regime Beta? From a control systems feedback perspective, the answer is that the presence of ice strongly altered the amplification effect. Recall that an ice-free region would typically have an albedo of approximately 0.1. Recall also that ice coverage would elevate surface albedo to approximately 0.9. Therefore, the amplification of what is called the gain between the presence or absence of ice was approximately ninefold.

Note that in Regime Alpha and Regime Gamma the amplification was effectively zero. It was only during Regime Beta that ice could so strongly impact Earth's albedo and hence its radiation balance. Of course, this train of logic requires an as-yet unproven fact: that Earth's mantle shifted cyclically as Earth's obliquity shifted. I will leave it for future researchers to investigate this hypothesis.

I conjecture that the termination of Regime Beta occurred when Earth's temperature became sufficiently cold to cause permanent ice coverage on the two poles.

As I said, this is merely a conjecture, and admittedly a flimsy one. However, I am not aware of any other attempt to provide another explanation of why the 41K periodicity cycles appear only in Regime Beta, and strongly at that.

There is a second possibility that might explain the origination and termination of Regime Beta. Specifically, the dynamic mechanism that altered the position of Earth's mantle relative to the spin axis could have been initiated and then been terminated.

Of the two proposed conjectures, I consider the former the most plausible. We humans know little about the dynamics of the planet as an object tumbling about in space with a sizeable molten core. Moreover, the molten core is largely composed of iron which can shift in position based on magnetic interactions, such as with other heavenly bodies.

In summary, Regime Alpha was much warmer than today but gradually cooling, Regime Beta was characterized by 41K year cycles with more gradual cooling, and Regime Gamma exhibits 100K year periods with a sawtooth pattern.

Why Bodies of Water Flip

A PHRASE I WILL USE AGAIN IS: The Earth hides its secrets well. This idea applies to bodies of water, both freshwater and seawater, that overturn. One common trait is the abruptness of an overturning.

Although these events are not common, history provides some accounts of bodies of water—mostly freshwater—that have overturned. Lake Monoun in West Province, Cameroon, overturned on August 14, 1984 [11]. The overturning was abrupt, happening at night within a span of several hours. It was accompanied by the degassing of the lake, a sort of Earthly belch, where a dense cloud of toxic gases hung over the lake. This cloud, being denser than the surrounding air, stayed close to ground level and migrated beyond the lake, resulting in the deaths of 37 nearby residents, all due to asphyxiation.

In one instance, toxic gases enveloped a truck, and the truck's engine stalled owing to the lack of oxygen. The dozen occupants within the truck all perished. Interestingly, two riders were on top of the truck, something apparently common in the area. Those two riders survived as their elevated position prevented their asphyxiation. Several years later, in 1986, a more violent overturning and eruption occurred in Lake Nyos in Cameroon.

The point is that gases released in an overturning are commonly denser than the surrounding air and remain close to the ground—and are localized. Then, wind and natural diffusion processes will disperse the released toxic gases.

Our knowledge of the mechanics that cause flipping and violent overturning of lakes is limited, however, three things are typical: (i) when an overturning occurs, it's abrupt, (ii) the overturning includes a degassing of the lake, and (iii) owing to the dynamic action of the movement of deep water as it upwells, tsunami-type waves strike the shorelines. In the case of Lake Nyos, for example, reports indicate that the resulting wave action caused tsunami waves estimated to be 19 meters (about 62 feet) tall. Should any body of water become unstable and thus overturn, the magnitudes of the waves created are significant.

My purpose in discussing the overturning of Lake Nyos is not to answer questions related to climate and climate dynamics, but rather to provide a better understanding of the physics related to bodies of water that overturn. In my estimation, the events associated with Lake Nyos serve as a testimony to the importance of bodies of water and their stability properties.

An otherwise quiet deep lake, Lake Nyos "flipped" on the night of August 21, 1986. A resultant gas cloud of immense proportions asphyxiated 1,746 nearby sleeping residents and approximately

3,000 head of cattle and other livestock.

The photograph below shows Lake Nyos following its lethal degassing and overturning. Anyone enjoying a midnight swim would have perished. No human would have survived.

The reddish color was said to have resulted from sediments that came upward as the lake overturned in its violent upheaval.

Lake Nyos

Although not evident in the above photograph, waves and rising waters covered adjacent land well beyond the lake's original shoreline. The rising muddied waters and waves left silt deposits above the shoreline.

The mass of gases released was extensive enough to lower the lake's level by approximately one meter in the overnight event.

The photograph above below just some of the thousands of asphyxiated animals. The cause of the Lake Nyos overturning has not yet been established.

Aftermath of Lake Nyos Overturning

The Lake Nyos degassing event serves as a vivid demonstration that even pretty oceans and serene lakes can at times become violent and deadly—and with little warning. Local legend had it that Lake Nyos had been stable for approximately 300 years or longer prior to its deadly 1986 overturning. I conjecture that the Lake Nyos overturning and subsequent degassing were not related to any astronomical forcing activity or mechanism.

The flipping of a body of water can occur due to varied candidate mechanisms. The most prevalent cause of overturning is a density inversion. When bodies of water flip because of a density inversion, the upper layer of water has become denser than the deeper water. Density inversions cause instability, which can result in an overturning. When the deep water rises in the upwelling, the rapid decrease in hydrostatic pressure in turn causes the dissolved gases, such as carbon dioxide and methane, to come out of solution, thus forming gas bubbles that rise.

Various types of liquid bodies experience inversions and overturning. One common example is sewage treatment plant lagoons. During most of the year, cooler, denser water remains at depth, while the warmer water stays at the surface. As the temperature decreases during the fall and the surface water of the sewage lagoon cools, the deeper water rises and mixes with the cooling surface water. The overturn releases odorous compounds into the atmosphere, which is why regulations specify that sewage ponds be located downwind and away from dwellings.

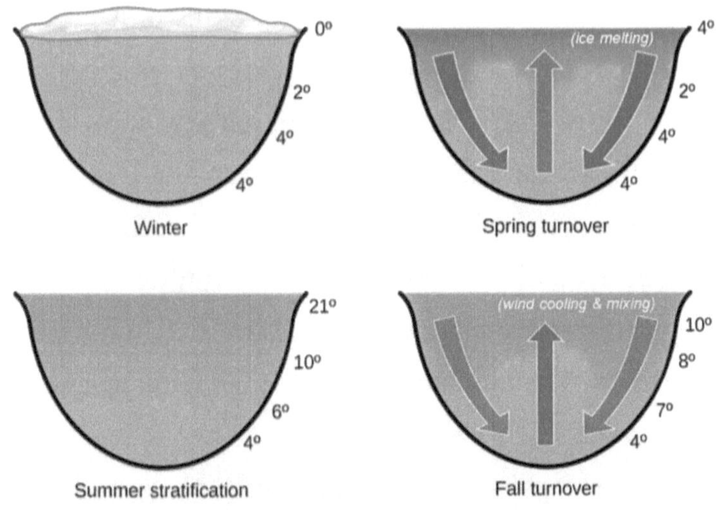

Typical Sewage Lagoon Overturning Cycle [12]

With a density inversion, it's not necessary to have a triggering action. Like gravity, it doesn't require a trigger.

A second candidate mechanism might be plausible: Supersaturation of the water with gases can lead to formation of gas bubbles, which then rise. The saturation limit of any liquid—its ability to hold dissolved gases— varies with temperature and is also influenced by pressure. As a general rule, the current literature focuses on the role played by dissolved gases, notably carbon dioxide. Liquids can, at times, go into a condition that chemists call supersaturated, and this warrants discussion of triggering mechanisms. Gaseous discharges that can be triggered by increases in deep water temperatures, mechanical agitation, or other means are called limnic eruptions. Many researchers who focus on limnic eruptions place heavy emphasis on the role of carbon dioxide in the overturning of bodies of water. They infer that some type of triggering mechanism is required, which may hold true in this case.

In contrast, gravity itself responds to correct any condition that is unstable. It's axiomatic in control systems theoretic principles that any process or state that is unstable serves as its own triggering mechanism. Of course, if an external trigger acts upon any unstable condition, this action will accelerate the dynamics. In the case of a density inversion, if a triggering action should occur, this obviously hastens the dynamics seeking a new equilibrium. Once the upwelling and associated gas release start the bubble formation process, the upward movement of the released gas bubbles accelerates the flip.

A third mechanism that might lead to a body of water overturning is temperature. When water is at or close to the saturation limit, should the temperature rise even slightly, a degassing of the water may occur.

In the case of Lake Nyos, it has also been suggested that dissolved gas accumulation at depth was related to subsurface mantle venting. Lake Nyos was formed as a volcanic crater lake, therefore, gases from the mantle could seep into its lowest depths. It's possible that a supersaturation condition of these dissolved gases at some depth may have initiated the degassing and resultant upwelling of the lake.

One article speculates another potential cause of the Lake Nyos degassing to be a possible below-surface rockslide, triggering the eruption because of implied mechanical agitation [13]. I tend to discount the rockslide conjecture, but it nonetheless rests in the plausible category.

My central purpose in discussing Lake Nyos is not to solve the mystery, but instead to make the reader aware of a well-documented, relatively recent overturning of a body of water.

Another observation seems warranted. When I suggest the possibility of an ocean overturning event, I have deliberately avoided stating which ocean layers might be impacted. Because the available climate records suggest that the rise in CO_2 concentration is both slow and modest, this leads me towards a hypothetical overturning scenario wherein only certain layers of the ocean participate in the overturning. My suspicion is that any overturning does not involve deep ocean water; I conjecture that the overturning involves only the mixing layer. The idea that deep ocean waters overturn, thus causing abrupt climatic change, is not supported by the available temperature histories. If indeed deep ocean waters would upwell, the impact on Earth's climate would be more pronounced and clearly reflected in the temperature record.

Having discussed varied candidate mechanisms that can cause or contribute to overturning, I am comfortable asserting a density inversion for the ocean overturning mechanism in my hypothesis, as a density inversion is the most likely candidate to cause the regular, periodic overturnings. It is unlikely that a rockslide or volcanic gas leak could happen with such regularity as to produce what we see in the established climate record.

Future hydrologists and climatologists can write dissertations to settle the matter; I state my hypothesis relying on my intuition and instincts, after taking the available climate record into account.

Avoiding Snowball Earth

WAY BACK IN OUR CLIMATE HISTORY, there is some evidence that the planet was in a snowball Earth scenario. One source used the date of approximately 660 million years ago [14]. There is considerable debate even today as to whether such a scenario ever existed. If it did exist, what brought it about? And then, what caused the Earth to somehow break out of that cold grip of ice? My discussion is not intended to address those questions.

For us today, one central and perplexing question emerges: Why has our planet not gone, at least in the last 100M years or so, into a similar frozen snowball condition?

Using my feedback systems training and instincts, my educated guess is that the descent into the glaciation is precisely because the Earth is driving itself towards a snowball scenario. A host of positive feedbacks appear to have been active at various times to drive our climate system in that direction. There would appear to be little opposition. What then causes the abrupt reversal? Why does the Earth appear to bounce back out of the grips of an ice age?

I doubt many would argue that an ocean overturning would be the ultimate game changer in impacting the Earth's climate. However, getting people to agree with me that the ocean indeed flipped every 100K years, such as in Regime Gamma, is a vastly harder challenge.

It would be fair to say that the acceptance or rejection of my hypothesis boils down to addressing the following five questions:

1. Does (or did) the ocean(s) become unstable and thus flip?
2. Is it conceivable that such overturning could be cyclical and thus display a 100K year periodicity?
3. Is the flipping self-generating, or is the action of an external driver or trigger required?
4. Is this ocean overturning the cause of the Earth's temperature rebound?
5. What role, if any, did the breakup and melting of the sea ice play in causing the abrupt climate reversal?

The answer to the first question must be affirmative if one thing can be proved: The ocean developed a density inversion during the glacial maxima of sufficient magnitude to initiate the overturning.

The density of seawater depends largely on three things: pressure, salinity, and temperature.

It's reasonable to assume that seawater behaves as an incompressible liquid, thus its density varies only minutely with the pressures that would be applicable in oceans. As such, I disregarded the role of pressure in determining the density of seawater.

As for salinity, I made the assumption that it did not vary appreciably as it pertains to ocean overturning. Ocean salinity generally falls within a very small range.

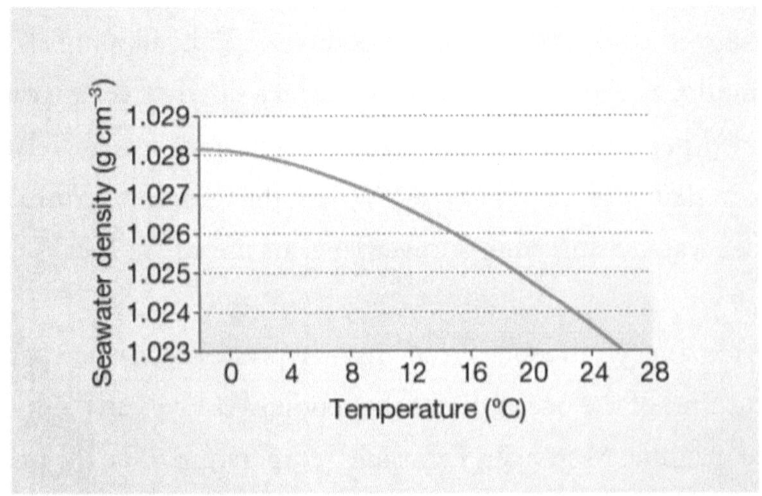

Seawater Density Variation with Temperature Changes

That leaves us with temperature. Upon examination of the above figure, I find it interesting that for seawater, the maximum density coincides with the freezing point. In contrast, distilled or pure water has a maximum density somewhat above the freezing point, at about 4 degrees Celsius, assuming atmospheric pressure.

Clearly, for the greater part, oceans remain stable. The one exception comes, if my hypothesis is valid, when the upper ocean layer chills, or conversely, the deeper layers warm. If salinity isn't a factor, the temperature profile would be the dominant property determining density. If the coldest water is near the surface, it would follow that the density inversion would have been created.

Now that we've addressed how and when a density inversion

occurs (i.e. the first question in the list), I will answer the remaining questions. The density inversion is the result of the Earth's temperature dropping to the freezing point for a long enough period that the top layers of the ocean are chilled while the bottom layers are warmer. The amount of time this takes is consistent, resulting in the 100K year periodicity. This flipping is self-generating, as a result of the ocean's surface slowly freezing over an extended period of time while the lower waters remain relatively warmer than the upper layers. When the ocean overturns, the warmer water rising from a lower layer of the ocean breaks up the sea ice.

I remain confident about my hypothesis that a periodic overturning of the ocean drives the rebound of the Earth out of the glacial maxima. Moreover, I consider temperature to be the primary mechanism in determining the density profile of the ocean as a function of depth. It is through these mechanisms that Earth has avoided becoming one giant snowball.

Radiation as a Heat Transfer Mechanism

The climate record in Regime Gamma is clear on one point: Periodic sudden events took place within each 100K year cycle, at the same approximate time relative to each cycle. These sudden events altered the Earth's radiation balance. Clearly, whatever caused the climate change also drove radiation change. As we'll see, radiation plays an important role in the climate cycle.

Simply stated, heat transfer has three modes: conduction, convection, and radiation. Mechanical engineering students typically learn this in the first few lectures of their first undergraduate course in heat transfer.

So which of these specific mechanisms cause heat to move, i.e. the "transfer" part of "heat transfer"?

We can eliminate conduction and convection from our discussion right off the bat. The Earth, as a body orbiting the sun, does so in the vacuum of space. The Earth cannot conduct heat, either away from or to itself. Convection isn't able to add or remove heat from the Earth. Conduction and convection simply do not apply to a vacuum. (These mechanisms do apply, however, to heat as it moves within the confines of the planet.)

So, in terms of Earth's interactions with the solar system and the cosmos, we are left with radiation. Given the available data, I will make the logical presumption to set aside the external drivers that might contribute to inbound radiation fluctuations. Yes, I am aware that insolation (solar flux) is somewhat cyclical and/or variable, but the magnitude in its variations is believed to be relatively weak [15]. Moreover, as far as is known, the frequencies associated with insolation fluctuations fail to coincide with the 100K year climate cycle of interest.

With all else eliminated, we are left to explore internal drivers of radiation fluctuations. One such driver is albedo, which I'll cover next.

The Albedo Effect

I'VE MENTIONED ALBEDO A FEW TIMES—now let's dive deeper into the albedo effect.

Albedo (reflectivity) is a dimensionless number. It ranges from 0, representing a black body with no reflectivity, up to 1.0, that being a body that reflects all incoming radiation back and away.

Ice coverage during the glacial maxima causes the Earth's albedo to be much greater than its present value of about 30 percent, or 0.30. I've seen a different source use the value of 0.37 [15]. In order to compute some numbers, I will take the conservative value and use 0.37 for the Earth's present-day albedo. That means that 37 percent of all inbound solar radiation is currently bounced away from Earth and reflected back into space. Consequently, this leaves only about 63 percent of the sun's solar radiation that strikes the Earth to be absorbed by Earth.

When the ice sheets are at their maximum reach (as in an ice age during Regime Gamma), the albedo for all of Earth on average is considerably higher because an ice-covered region has a greater reflectivity. In contrast, open ocean water (like we have today) absorbs up to 90 percent of solar radiation, especially in the lower latitudes when the sun is more overhead (thereby closer to its zenith).

The Albedo Scale below shows the percentage of diffusely reflected sunlight relative to various surface conditions [16].

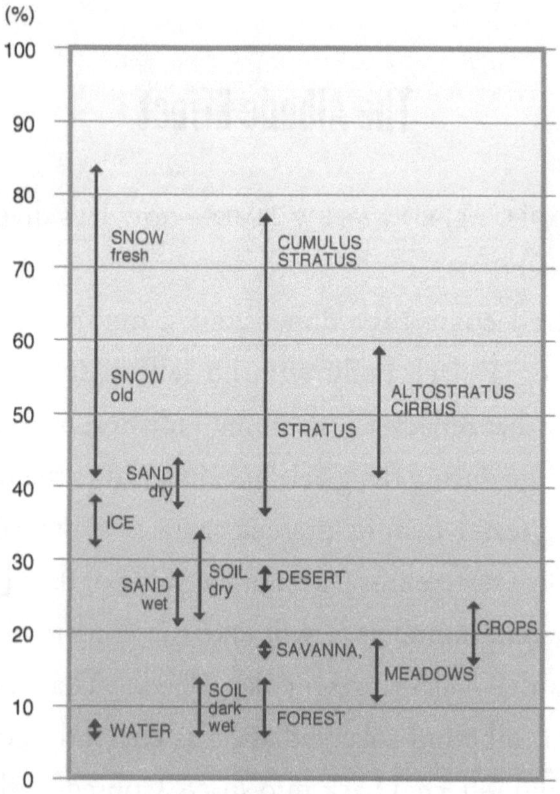

The Albedo Scale

At the higher latitudes, the sun's ability to warm the Earth is decreased for two reasons: (i) the lower angle of the sun relative to the horizon means that less solar radiation impacts each unit of surface area, and (ii) at low angles of incoming radiation the water is more reflective. Think of it like skipping stones that can ricochet off water when the impact angle is low.

In stark contrast to open water, ice is far more reflective of inbound solar radiation. During a period of glacial maxima, the ice covering the Earth (including sea ice on the ocean surface) absorbs only about 10 percent of the incoming solar radiation. Thus, about 90 percent of the sun's radiation striking ice gets reflected back into space.

Based on this reasoning and a few back-of-the-envelope calculations, I estimate the Earth's albedo at the time of the glacial maxima in Regime Gamma to be approximately 0.6, or 60 percent. Consequently, the retained energy from the inbound solar radiation is reduced to about 40 percent. Since today's albedo is .37, that means 37 percent of the radiation is reflected away, so the amount absorbed is 63 percent. This is significantly greater than the 40 percent of inbound radiant energy retained during the glacial maxima. Sixty-three percent of incoming energy being cut down to forty percent represents a whopping drop, about one-third, in the net solar radiation retained by Earth.

It's important to underscore the magnitude of albedo and its strong positive feedback nature. Albedo feeds upon itself, thus having the capability of pushing the planet into a steadily colder, snowball Earth scenario. The role of albedo is certainly important, but it is also noteworthy that many of the proposed theories ignore albedo and instead focus on a simple correlation argument.

Expertise in Feedback Systems Theory

THOUSANDS, IF NOT TENS OF THOUSANDS, of articles on climate dynamics exist, but I see no reason to discuss the available literature. It suffices for me to presume the question of glacial causation is unresolved and try to resolve it using what I know best—feedback system theoretic principles—and treating Earth's climate as a closed loop feedback system. The theory I arrived at holds on its own, regardless of the existing literature on climate change. I have operated within the rules of science, where the starting point of any scientific inquiry is the conjecture, or hypothesis, as an attempt to answer the "why" question.

In my graduate education I was introduced to theoretic principles in mathematics and feedback systems theory. I became intrigued with the concept of limit cycles. As I explained previously, limit cycles are self-generating and are not caused by external drivers. They occur only in systems containing nonlinearities. Everyday examples of limit cycles include machine tool chatter, thermostats, and how vehicle braking systems pulsate when brakes are subject to anti-skid control.

When I entered academia as an assistant professor, I was free to research topics of my choosing. I was once given a t-shirt with a quotation attributed to me. The quotation read simply, "I am a solution in search of a problem."

Me Wearing My Favorite Shirt

My theoretical background in the mathematics of unexplained oscillating or cyclical objects led me to study climate dynamics. I have no specific certification to study Earth's climate dynamics but no license is required to study it. I am not a licensed Professional Engineer as during my working career, California was the only state that licensed engineers in Control Systems—my specialization—and I have never practiced in California.

As a researcher without grants or external funding, I studied climate dynamics as a personal pursuit. For me it was a matter of seeking truth. Some people solve crossword puzzles, some do knitting and embroidery as their recreation. I chose to unravel the climate change mystery. Although I have devoted much time pursuing the glacial causation question, I delayed writing on the topic as other projects took higher priority:

• Development of an international program for teaching bicycle skills to children with disabilities [17]

• Researching sway control methodologies for skyscrapers [18]

Once I retired, I was able to focus my attention on glacial causation. In the grand scheme of 90,000 years, what was another 50?

Background in Mechanical Engineering

WHY AM I QUALIFIED TO AUTHOR THIS BOOK? Well, it helps that I have three earned degrees in mechanical engineering.

It is said that mechanical engineering is the forefather of engineering. Mechanical engineering came first, emerging as the industrial revolution came on the world scene. The heart of the industrial revolution was the steam engine. Prior to the steam engine, mankind's quest for power was limited to animal power, human slaves at times, and wind/water power. Energy was scarce. Water sources of energy were geographically fixed. Windmills cropped up in windy areas, but windmills weren't easily moved. Likewise, mills powered by water were required to be located where water was falling.

Then a significant advance occurred. Steam engines were invented by Thomas Newcomen and others, but for almost a century, they were both inefficient and cantankerous. While visiting in Scotland in 1764, James Watt became fascinated with steam engines and devised several significant improvements. In 1787, Watt introduced a device called the flyball governor. The technology regarding flyball governors had actually been known for several centuries in controlling the speed of windmills. Although it's often claimed that James Watt invented the steam engine, his contribution was to make power generation by the burning of fuels practical. The advent of the steam engine also permitted the source of mechanical power to be portable. History tells the story of how all of mankind was impacted by the steam-powered industrial revolution.

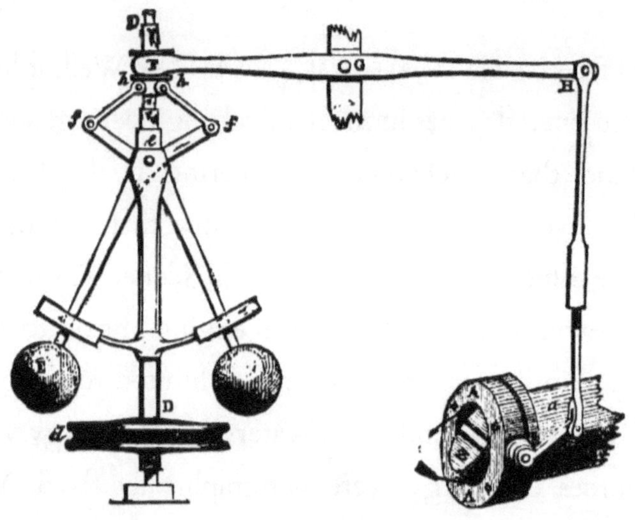

Flyball Governor

In 1868, James Clark Maxwell authored a treatise titled "On Governors" [19], whereby Maxwell reduced the analysis of flyball governor dynamics to a problem in mathematics, notably differential equations. Although feedback systems were preexisting in nature as well as having been improvised by humans, it was

Maxwell's analysis and writings that ushered in the era of feedback control systems.

Interestingly, the goal of a feedback systems theoretician is not to solve problems *per se*, but rather to bound the feedback system's output options. Contributors along the way included E.J. Routh, Heinrik Bode, and H. Nyquist. The focus of the works by these three giants was twofold: (i) to bound the problem in terms of answering the stability question, and (ii) to provide synthesis techniques whereby a system's closed loop feedback response could be improved.

As World War II loomed, the development of feedback principles, also referred to as servomechanisms, increased. Note that the word servomechanism is derived from the Latin-based word servo, implying slave or servant. Hence, a machine or device was able to do the work formerly done by beasts of burden, servants, or slaves.

In the late 1930s, President Roosevelt realized, and wisely so, that the United States would be drawn into the war already raging in Europe. He sensed that WWII was going to be a long war, and one that would ultimately be won or lost hinging on technology.

With this vision, Roosevelt appointed the most capable man he could identify to head up the United States' technological war efforts: Dr. Vannevar Bush (1890-1974). Roosevelt and Bush were wealthy men who frequented similar social circles. Both of them sailed yachts off of the coast of Rhode Island.

By profession, Bush was an electrical engineer. At the time, he was the Dean of Engineering at the Massachusetts Institute of Technology (MIT). It is little wonder that MIT became the focal point of our nation's technological war efforts. Bush headed the combined work of about 6,000 mathematicians, engineers, and scientists who gave our nation things like radar, Loran navigation, inertial navigation (improved gyroscopes), improved vacuum tubes, code breaking, and advances in servomechanisms.

Roosevelt was correct in his predictions that the war would be long as well as waged and won with technology. Feedback control systems were foundational in the war effort, and the body of mathematical techniques expanded greatly during WWII.

The servomechanisms developments in America during WWII had been based largely on what is called the frequency domain. That came about because of the research of mathematician Dr. Harold Nyquist and electrical engineers Hendrik W. Bode and Harold S. Black in the 1920s and 1930s at Bell Telephone Laboratories.

The experimental work at Bell Telephone was based on frequency response excitation. The Nyquist Criterion, a mathematical theorem, solidified experimental findings regarding amplifier stabilization [20]. The techniques for telephone transmission stabilization developed prior to the war were adopted and transported to help solve war-related problems like servomechanism positioning of large naval gun turrets. Hydraulics were used to accurately aim large naval guns on ships at sea. Feedback principles were applied to the servosystem reactions of ships to maintain accuracy of the gun despite the pitching and rolling of the vessel at sea. The mathematical techniques developed at Bell Telephone Laboratories assured the performance and the stability of the closed-loop positioning mechanisms. Thus, the pattern governing the future became clear: Massive objects can be controlled and stabilized by feedback loops of information.

Advances made during the war paved the way for solving broader classes of problems in industry. These post-war contributions focused on feedback theory centered on frequency domain solution techniques.

The West did not know of Soviet advances until well after WWII when Soviet works were translated and made available. The Soviet advances in feedback control systems came from mathematicians, whereas the American developments were heavily influenced by the electrical engineers at Bell Laboratories. The Soviet launch of Sputnik on October 4, 1957 added more impetus for America to get its high-tech house in order.

The matrix algebra approach coming out of American universities was popularized by the work of Dr. Rudolph E. Kálmán (1930-2016). Kálmán's ideas contributed to the rapid progress of systems theory, which today draws upon mathematics ranging from differential equations to algebraic geometry [21].

The high-speed digital computer became increasingly viable as circuitry, chips, transistors, and solid-state devices emerged along with advances in computer memory. The ability to perform high-speed repetitive calculations permitted the automation of time-domain control systems.

In the two decades following the close of the war, the field of feedback control systems, previously known as servomechanisms, solidified. The Soviet and American approaches merged to become a unified body of knowledge. The principles and practices of feedback control systems became an important part of engineering educational curricula.

Mechanical engineering, the king of all branches of engineering, can be thought of as a three-legged stool: (i) the thermodynamics of steam, (ii) the design and thus kinematics of the components, and (iii) the role played by the mathematics of feedback systems theoretic principles.

I obtained both my MS and PhD degrees in feedback control systems theory during the emergence of this field. Interestingly, accreditation requirements for U.S. mechanical engineering programs were changed at that time to include coursework in feedback systems theory. As one of the few doctorates in feedback systems at that time, my telephone rang off the hook. I received job offers from numerous universities to teach control systems theory, with some offers made over the phone and without even a site visit. I was blessed to be in the right place at the right time.

Image of Pyramids Courtesy of National Geographic

The industrial revolution, built on the foundation of mechanical engineering, transformed the world. The world prior to the industrial revolution was typified by enslavement and forced labor of peoples. One example is the great pyramids of Egypt. Each pyramid took decades to build and consumed many lives. Historians speculate that each pyramid required as many as 100,000 workers.

Another example is the Roman empire. As the Romans conquered foreign lands, the people within were commonly forced into slavery. Galley ships were powered by chained slaves pulling at oars. Slavery was far more the norm than the exception. The population of the Roman empire included so many slaves that threats of a slave uprising were constant.

Sometimes people would even sell themselves or their children into slavery to resolve debts or avoid starvation.

In China, the construction of the Great Wall took several thousand years and consumed an estimated million enslaved workers who died.

Image of the Great Wall of China Courtesy of National Geographic

Then the Newcomb steam engine—along with James Watt's improvements to efficiency—changed the world. The advent of the industrial revolution diminished the importance of slavery as an institution. New machinery was able to generate power that humans could not.

The role of mechanical engineering, and feedback systems principles in particular, cannot be overstated. Controlling any device is a paramount achievement that implicitly requires that stability be achieved and maintained. Devices that lack stability will self-destruct. And yet, the principles foundational to feedback systems and their importance are commonly overlooked.

As I pondered the "why" question underlying climate changes, I viewed the problem through the lens of these feedback control systems principles. I like to compare feedback systems to a black hole. Those standing from afar look in but see nothing. My goal is to bring light where previously there was darkness.

I am egotistical enough to think that I have come up with a handful of worthy ideas over my lifetime. I suppose that being egotistical goes hand-in-hand with being creative, otherwise people such as inventors, actors, poets, etc. would produce nothing. The drive that causes someone to build a better mouse trap inherently stems from the inventor's inner belief that he or she can do it better than anyone else has before that point.

I recall a quotation that bears on this, "… but like all Inventors, every goose to him represents a swan" [22]. Inventors may overestimate the worth of their invention, but again, that comes with the territory. If the inventor wasn't infatuated with an idea, it would never have become an invention in the first place.

Thus, being able to tackle a complex problem like climate change requires creativity, critical thinking, and some measure of egotism. Good thing I have all three.

OTHER THEORIES AND IDEAS

"I shiver, thinking how easy it is to be totally wrong about people—to see one tiny part of them and confuse it for the whole, to see the cause and think it's the effect or vice versa."
~ Lauren Oliver

Five Screening Tests to Evaluate the Theories

ALTHOUGH I HAVEN'T PERFORMED AN ACTUAL COUNT, I believe 60 or more glacial causation theories have been proposed. In the discussion by Sergin & Sergin [23], they assert that the number of proposed theories exceeds 100. The bulk of those have been refuted.

Science is not subject to a vote. The majority does not rule. Truth is the sole goal, the thing pursued. The challenge is to state a hypothesis and then validate the hypothesis.

Many researchers have made earnest attempts to put forth an adequate hypothesis, but no theory as of yet has been validated. The numerous attempted glacial explanations simply have no merit.

Many believe that cyclical ice age causation can be easily explained by their correlation to Milankovitch cycles. Despite this widespread belief, I consider Milankovitch cycle explanations to be lacking, especially as the sole driver of glacial causation. The earth sciences community has yet to successfully identify Earth's glacial causation mechanism.

Admittedly, solutions to climate-related questions are not easily proved. Rejection of a proposed theory is by far easier. To evaluate the proposed glacial causation theories, I have found five tests to be useful as screening mechanisms. Note that all of these tests have a major weakness: Although failure to pass will exclude a candidate theory, surviving the tests does not necessarily prove the theory to be valid. Despite that weakness, these tests are able to identify and thus eliminate some of the flawed theories. It's still possible for a flawed theory to remain until disproven by some other test or argument.

To date, the majority of extant glacial causation theories have been weeded out by application of these five tests. The theoretical argument posed by Ellis & Palmer [24] is somewhat unique, having been reported on following peer review. I'll address the Ellis & Palmer work in a subsequent chapter.

Here are the five screening tests:

1. **Causality:** The cause must come before the effect, certainly not the other way around.

2. **Abruptness and jaggedness:** The theory must be able to support the abrupt rise in temperature coming out of the ice age (as it applies to the Regime Gamma period with the 100K year cycles) alongside the fact that this regularly happens in multiple steps, creating a jagged line upward.

3. **Regularity:** The theory must adequately explain the regularity in timing of both the 100K year cycles and the 41K year cycles.

4. **Emergence of 41K year cycles:** The theory must support the transition at three million YBP from a relatively smooth climate history with only modest and higher frequency variations over

to a history with a predominant 41K year cycle.

5. **Frequency change compatibility:** The theory should be compatible with the frequency change from 41K year cycles over to 100K year cycles, which occurred approximately one million years before present.

The fifth screening test, related to the change in frequency, is of considerable utility; applying only this fifth test allowed me to eliminate a large number of candidate theories.

Theories Based on External Drivers

THE BULK OF CURRENT GLACIAL CAUSATION THEORIES, with two exceptions (to my knowledge), are based on the presumption of an external driver, some sort of forcing mechanism or external triggering action. It's tempting to view the situation as a simple two-step process. The first step is to identify an external driver that has the same base frequency as the observed climate fluctuations. The second step is to conclude that driver X is the causation of the observed cycle Z.

Such logic isn't good science. The similar frequencies can be merely a coincidence. In order to establish credibility, a crucial requirement must be met: The causation mechanism of the driver needs to be identified.

Of the extant climate theories, astronomically based theories are by far the most prevalent. Others seek to link the Earth's climate cycles to geological activity. Some of the explanations are based on factors such as:

- changes in solar insolation (changes in the amount of incoming sunlight)
- a cyclical or pulsating sun
- cyclical orbit changes (suggested by Milankovitch roughly a century ago)
- periodic volcanic activity
- periodic impacting of our solar system with interstellar gas and/or dust clouds
- the sinking of the Earth's mantle in localized regions due to the immense weight of glacial ice buildup in various regions
- continental drift or other shifting of the Earth's tectonic plates
- lifting of the Tibetan plateau (thus changing the snow line and hence the reflectivity properties above the snow line)
- an as-yet-unknown comet that hypothetically visits our solar system every 100,000 years

To date, no proposed theory has stood up to the challenges raised against it.

Perhaps the most absurd theory concerns the invisible hand of some unseen comet or interstellar gas and/or dust cloud. The theory states that a comet or gas/dust cloud comes and goes and thus causes the changes in Earth's climate record. The proponents of this theory believe so strongly in it that I've heard they even named the unseen extraterrestrial object.

If one were to argue in favor of a 100K year cyclical astronomical driver, it would suggest that some extraterrestrial or astronomical event happened within the cosmos one million years ago that caused orbits and comets to change abruptly. In my view, this is highly improbable. Even more improbable is that these cycles would continue to be regular following this event—either that an astronomical event would continue to occur approximately every 100K years or that these regular 100K year cycles would continue on their own without any further astronomical intervention.

Another trait associated with astronomically driven events concerns precision in timing. It is said that time and tide wait for no man. Tides function with precision—their timing is quite precise and predictable. Analogously, astronomically driven events tend to occur with precision in timing. Although the 100K year cyclical glaciations have a basic rhythm, the attribute of preciseness isn't present. The periodic glaciations, both in Regime Beta and Regime Gamma, flunk the precision-in-timing test.

Due to these lines of thinking, I have eliminated all extraterrestrial and astronomical drivers as the cause of the glacial cyclic oscillations.

My primary reason for rejecting both astronomical and also geological theories relates to the shift in observed frequencies in the climate record. The shift from 41K year cycles to 100K year cycles, which took place approximately one million YBP, is contradictory and just not in keeping with systems driven by a presumed periodic and unchanging external driver. If we believe there was an external, periodic, unchanging astronomical or geological force that caused the initial 41K year cycle, then by necessity the subsequent 100K year cycles couldn't have happened because that would have required a change to the driver. Because the 100K year cycles did happen, we can conclude that the 41K year cycles were not caused by a periodic, unchanging force.

Of course, one could argue that an astronomical driver mechanism exists that is (or was) aperiodic in nature, i.e. irregular or not periodic. Some even argue that some as-of-yet unseen and unexplained aperiodic driver is responsible for the Alpha, Beta, and Gamma records. Such an attempted explanation is preposterous. How could something so aperiodic result in something with such a regular rhythm? I flatly reject all external driver theories, including any with aperiodic behavior.

To compound matters, virtually all current astronomical and geological theories fail to pass the second test of abruptness: Compatibility with the Earth's sudden climb out of the glacial eras during the most recent one million years, as evident in Regime Gamma. An external driver, including cyclical astronomical theories, would not cause a rapid temperature rebound, certainly not at the same approximate timing within each of the respective 100K year cycles. Moreover, it is implausible that an astronomical driver would have been responsible for the discrete stair-step temperature rebound.

If astronomical and/or geological drivers truly caused ice ages, the temperature record would be far less abrupt in its rebound and far more gradual. Also, if astronomical or geological drivers were responsible, then the climate record would display consistency of cyclical behavior. In causal systems involving slowly changing capacitances, the presence of an input only under the rarest of conditions would produce an abrupt change in a system's forced response.

The fact that the abrupt rebound is a characteristic of each of the 100K year cycles (those occurring within the most recent one million years, in the Regime Gamma), allowed me to dismiss the plausibility of a one-time event. Whatever happened to cause the 100K year cycles must have also caused the abrupt rebound at the same predictable time within each cycle's interval.

The study of dynamic responses of nonlinear systems is indeed rich and interesting. Certain classes of nonlinear systems can exhibit what is known as jump resonance. A jump resonance occurs when a nonlinear system is being excited, such as being sinusoidally shaken [25]. When jump resonance occurs, the observed change in the resonance is in the form of a sudden or abrupt change in output amplitude. This does not appear to apply to the observed climate record as discussed for the past 5.5 million years. If jump resonance was happening, the change would only affect the amplitude of the resonant frequency as opposed to an abrupt change in the observed periodicity of resonance. As the climate record transitions from a relatively smooth temperature history in Regime Alpha to a 41K cyclical behavior in Regime Beta and then to an approximate 100K cyclical behavior in Regime Gamma, the abrupt change is in frequency and thus not merely a change in amplitude.

Of course, advocates of Milankovitch cycles would argue otherwise, saying that Milankovitch cycles explain periodic ice ages. As discussed earlier, Regime Beta is dominated by a descent in temperature along with 41K year cycles being superimposed. No proponents of Milankovitch cycles have explained why the 41K year cycles are observed in Regime Beta but not in Regime Alpha or Gamma. Also, advocates of Milankovitch cycles, including Ellis & Palmer, argue that the observed approximate 100K year cycles in Regime Gamma conform in occurrence with Milankovitch great summers. While that may be true, such advocates have not explained why Regime Alpha and Regime Beta lack synchronization with the cycles in Regime Gamma. I acknowledge that Milankovitch cycles may have an influence, however, something else in addition must be going on. I will return to this topic later.

Yet another oddity concerning the behavior of nonlinear systems concerns the topic of signal stabilization. It was observed that when a relatively high frequency signal was injected into a system exhibiting unwanted limit cycle behavior, the mere injection of the signal caused the unwanted limit cycle to die out. This experimental discovery has been credited to Dr. Rufus Oldenburger [26], who pursued the study of signal stabilization as a leading researcher at Purdue University. The fact that a limit cycle can appear and then seemingly vanish illustrates the complexity underlying nonlinear dynamics. I'm mentioning signal stabilization not to present it as a plausible explanation for or against glaciations, but rather to raise the potential for applicability in resolving climate dynamics.

With none of the theories based on external drivers passing the screening tests, we are ready to move on to theories based on internal drivers.

Theories Based on Internally Generated Cycles

BECAUSE APPLICATION OF THE FIVE SCREENING TESTS has eliminated such a wide array of external driver theories, I will now address whether an internally generated oscillation, essentially a closed-loop system, could provide a plausible glacial causation explanation. In mathematical terminology, this is a search for self-generating limit cycles. Limit cycles exist only in certain nonlinear systems. Some alternative names for nonlinear limit cycles are auto-oscillations and self-generated cycles or oscillations. Hunting, common in feedback systems with gears, is yet another name implying limit cycle behavior.

To date, I have identified only three internal or closed-system theories that have been put forth to explain climate cycles. I am the author and proponent of one such theory, one that I obviously embrace. The two other closed-system theories that I am aware of are the Sergin & Sergin work and the Ellis & Palmer work. Each has its own merit, so I will discuss each in their own chapter.

The Sergin & Sergin Work

SERGIN & SERGIN CONDUCTED EXTENSIVE STUDIES in the 1960s and 1970s focused on modeling Earth's climate dynamics. Over the span of a decade or more, they published numerous papers, presumably all in Russian. Sergin & Sergin were associated with the Pacific Institute of Geography, Vladivostok. In 1976, Sergin & Sergin published what appears to be a summary of much of their earlier work. This paper, in pamphlet form, investigated an internal, or closed-loop, dynamic systems mechanism. Sergin & Sergin published a second paper, "The System Analysis of the Problem of Large Variations of the Climate and Earth's Ice Ages," (in Russian), in 1978. I will treat both papers as one for discussion purposes, as I assume the sequel 1978 paper was issued mirroring the original 1976 summary to reach a broader readership.

In that 1976 summary, Sergin & Sergin described a nonlinear model of Earth's climate dynamic system. Each hemisphere of the Earth had its own model, and they provided for an algebraic linkage mechanism between the two hemispheric models. Each hemispheric model had three capacitances: ice resting on landmass, otherwise described as continental ice; the oceans; and the atmosphere. Because each hemisphere had three capacitances, the total model took into account six capacitances. The model examined heat interchanges associated with the three capacitances in each hemisphere. In thermodynamic terms, the heat energy associated with phase change is referred to as latent heat. Thus, the model addressed latent heat associated with the melting and refreezing of the ice caps and ice formations.

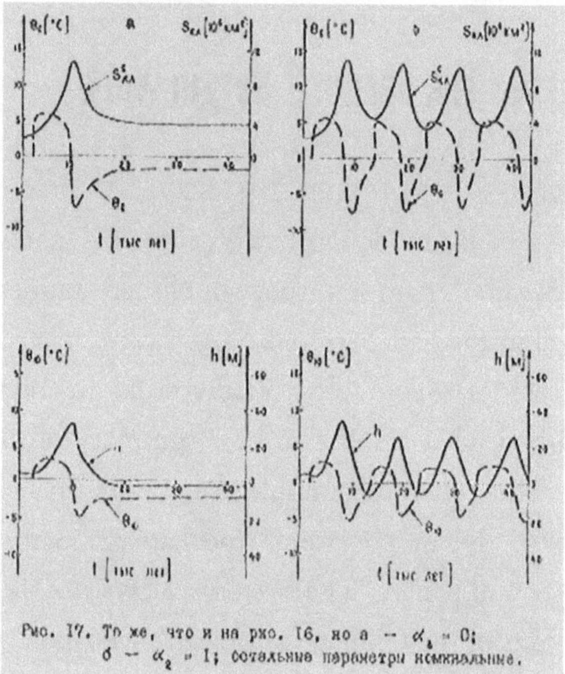

Image From Sergin & Sergin (analogue computer results)

Upper left: change in mean surface temperature in Northern Hemisphere
Upper right: area covered by continental ice
Lower left: change in mean surface temperature in Southern Hemisphere
Lower right: area covered by sea ice

The model described by Sergin & Sergin included varied nonlinear relationships and provisions for astronomical drivers, notably changes in Earth's orbit mechanics. Sergin & Sergin acknowledged that Milankovitch cycles, as forcing drivers, had the capacity for modulating effects on the model's outcomes. The Sergin & Sergin model made provisions whereby as ocean levels increased or decreased, the amount of exposed land versus sea area was taken into account.

Based on analogue computer simulations, the Sergin & Sergin model exhibited self-oscillation cycles over the recent Pleistocene. Prior warmer periods in Earth's climate history did not generate self-oscillations. Sergin & Sergin noted that the southern hemisphere as a model was stable and did not exhibit self-oscillating cyclical behavior. The analogue computer time histories generated by the Sergin & Sergin model for the northern hemisphere in the most recent Pleistocene did exhibit self-oscillation cycles, but these cycles only showed modified sawtooth behavior. The self-oscillations produced more rounded and less abrupt temperature rebounds. Depending on parameters assumed, the periods ranged between 20,000 and 80,000 years. The simulation model did not reproduce the 100,000 year cycles, but such a discrepancy has possible explanations. The difference in simulated periods is not a serious flaw as modeling goes. But because the Sergin & Sergin analogue simulations failed to produce abrupt rebounds in the most recent Pleistocene, it's reasonable to presume that the Sergin & Sergin modeling fails the abrupt rebound test.

As a feedback control systems theorist, I fully appreciate the efforts made by Sergin & Sergin to reduce the order of their mathematical model. One decision they made was to model the oceans as a single lumped parameter system. In other words, their model provided for a certain volume of seawater based on mean depth, surface area, and the assumption of a mixed capacitance. I view this assumption to be overly restrictive on the model's dynamic responses.

If the ocean instead had been modeled as a collection of horizontal slabs to represent the stratification of the ocean, then the dynamics as modeled would have been more faithful in replicating the realities of cyclical glaciations. In particular, the layering of horizontal slabs would have caused responses to be more delayed. Therefore, I hypothesize that two behaviors would have been impacted: (i) the period of self-oscillation would have been greater, and (ii) provisions for a density inversion would have simulated or provided for ocean overturning.

For over 40 years I lacked access to an English translation of the Sergin & Sergin work. Recently, an internet source provided an English translation [27].

In general, I was impressed with the modeling and mathematical proficiency displayed in the Sergin & Sergin work. As is typical with Russian sources, their skill in mathematics was noteworthy.

Because I had access to electronic analogue computing at the University of Illinois in the 1970s, I attempted to replicate the paper's analogue computer results.

Unfortunately, the paper lacked a tabulation of the parameters the authors had used, notably the amplifier gains, the potentiometer settings, and the nonlinear functions within the analogue computer model. Symbols contained in a simulation diagram meant little as I lacked the numerical values of these symbols. It is possible that the text in Russian provided the desired gains and nonlinear functions, but I could not read the Russian text. Without knowing the gains and such, I was unable to replicate the paper's findings.

Sergin & Sergin used their analogue computer model with skill to test a wide array of theories and parameter variations. For example, they caused Milankovitch, or astronomical, cycle dynamics to impact their climate model. Although the Milankovitch cycles did exhibit an impact, the effect was not dramatic.

As I bring my discussion of the Sergin & Sergin paper to a close, I must note its significance. Their work demonstrated a theory whereby a closed-loop phenomenon was argued. Sergin & Sergin also studied how external drivers, notably Milankovitch cycles, could influence the dynamics of cyclical glaciation causation. The dynamics were controlled based on self-oscillating arguments. But even when external drivers were introduced, self-oscillation remained as the dominant feature of cyclical glacial causation. Modulation may indeed impact timing, but the causation of the base cycle was internal to the mathematical model and thus self-generating. Modulation in no way constitutes grounds for a causality argument.

The Ellis & Palmer Hypothesis

ELLIS & PALMER (2016) hypothesized a hybrid argument concerning ice age causation. However, they discuss only ice age causation in the last 800K years and do not consider glacial causation dynamics or Earth's temperature variations prior to that.

Ralph Ellis is not a climatologist. He spent his career as a flight instructor and pilot, then after retiring reached out to Professor Michael Palmer, a chemist at the University of Waterloo in Canada. They wrote their peer-reviewed paper on climate despite having no documented history of prior climatology research. This is not a criticism, but rather an interesting observation. Within the scientific community, no regulations prevent outsiders from entering into a conversation.

The essence of the Ellis & Palmer work is a strictly theoretical argument with the goal of explaining cyclical glaciation causation. They have not conducted any experiments or made any attempts to develop computer simulations. As such, their work represents theoretical and yet creative thinking. Their work can be called hybrid because it involves both internal feedbacks and external driver mechanisms.

The internal feedback mechanism they outline argues that Earth's temperature and hence climate is, in large part, controlled by changes in Earth's albedo. To be specific:

• As the Earth cools, the cooling permits an increase in ice sheet coverage.

• Then, because ice sheets increase Earth's reflectivity or albedo, the Earth subsequently continues to cool down.

• As Earth's temperature drops, the temperature of the oceans' upper surface also drops. This is especially the case in the higher latitudes.

• Then, as surface water temperatures drop, the oceans become sinks for CO_2 absorption.

• The reduction in atmospheric CO_2 in turn causes higher plateau regions, notably the Gobi Desert or the Gobi plateau, to become deficient in atmospheric CO_2.

• Because atmospheric CO_2, especially in higher plateau regions, has dropped, this in turn creates a desert.

• As atmospheric CO_2 levels drop below critical levels, even grassy plants cease to grow.

• The high plateau regions, lacking in plants to stabilize the soil, become sources of atmospheric dust.

• At some point, the ice sheets acquire dirtiness. As dust layers form on the ice, this strongly reduces the albedo, thereby causing accelerated ice melting.

• As successive ice layers melt, the dust at the surface becomes reinforced. This is akin to ice becoming dirty once melting starts.

• The dirt and dust particles tend to remain in place, thereby causing a positive feedback mechanism which, in turn, accelerates the melting.

• As the ice sheets melt, more solar insolation is retained by Earth, causing Earth's atmospheric temperature to rise.

• The rise in atmospheric temperature thus establishes a warmer interglacial period.

The above steps are then poised to repeat themselves, thus providing an explanation for the cyclical glaciations experienced by Earth.

Interestingly, Ellis and Palmer discuss feedbacks, but they do not distinguish that feedbacks can be either positive or negative, or that negative feedbacks can be categorized as being either stable or unstable.

A key feature of the Ellis & Palmer work is how they account for the mechanism that causes Earth's temperature to suddenly rebound and emerge out of each glacial maxima. The Ellis & Palmer argument is modestly complex, but it's based on positive feedback principles.

The continued cooling of the Earth coming out of the warmer interglacial happens, as a hypothesis, because of positive feedback. As the Earth cools this, in turn, increases the spreading of ice sheets. As landmasses and even sea water become covered with increased ice sheets, Earth's albedo increases, thus increasing its reflectivity. In sum, the coldness brought about by positive feedback reinforces the coldness.

But then a seemingly abrupt reversal occurs. The climate record during the Pleistocene makes one point clear. After the Earth achieves glacial maxima conditions, it seems to stabilize, for a while at least, at a low temperature. Then something causes the Earth to rebound abruptly in temperature—but what is that "something"? Also note that during the Pleistocene, the rebounds exhibit a stair-stepping behavior. For example, as the Earth rebounded out of the last Wisconsin ice age about 12,000 years ago, the rebound occurred in three discrete steps.

It's the contention of Ellis and Palmer that the rebound out of a glacial maxima is based on dust accumulation from the higher plateau regions, particularly the Gobi Desert.

The heart of science is the skeptical mind. Although I have considerable respect for the theory and arguments advanced by Ellis and Palmer, my skepticism questions their dust theory. I argue that the action of dust in changing the albedo of any region covered by sheet ice is a microclimate phenomenon. It's hard to envision that the bulk of ice-covered regions, say in the northern hemisphere, all acted in rhythm. Moreover, because the Earth has rebounded out of approximately ten glacial maxima in the recent Pleistocene, the same mechanism would have had to replicate itself. Such an orchestrated happening seems highly improbable.

I see a second problem with the Ellis & Palmer dust rebound theory. Virtually all of the most recent ten rebounds in the Pleistocene were characterized by discrete step behavior. I argue that the Ellis & Palmer dust rebound hypothesis is incapable of explaining the presence of the discrete stair-like rebounds—their theory implies more of a smooth rebound.

The Ellis & Palmer work then argues that Milankovitch cycles serve as modulating mechanisms. The hypothesized functioning of the Milankovitch cycles, notably the great summer periods, permit the onset of the melt due to dust accumulation. This correlation may or may not be true in itself, but nothing in the dust theory or the Milankovitch modulation argument explains the discrete stair-step rebound behavior. Instead, we would still be seeking a temperature rebound mechanism that behaves in a macroclimate fashion. Like the one I proposed.

I have advanced a competing theory to the Ellis & Palmer theory. At present, science has its limitations. Other than conducting intellectual debates and what I call "arm waving," it is beyond our capability to validate or even disprove virtually any theory. The goal of reasonable persons is to seek out the truth. Ellis and Palmer could be right or they could be wrong. Likewise, Richard Klein could be right or he could be wrong. It is even possible that both arguments are wrong. Until some divine insights come to us, it is likely that the glacial causation question will remain unresolved. Yes, arriving at a solid answer would be great, but in the interim, it is incumbent upon all participants in the debate to remain of good cheer and display mutual respect.

In some regards, the Kleinian Glacial Causation Hypothesis bears a strong resemblance to the Ellis & Palmer hypothesis. Both are argued as a cyclical sequence of causality happenings. Both assume that when Earth is within an interglacial period, a positive feedback mechanism causes the planet to experience a temperature decline.

I have considerable admiration for the insights, theoretical ideas, and hard work by Ellis and Palmer. But I do fault the Ellis & Palmer work based on their language assertiveness. Throughout their work, they often make statements like "this is why" and proclaim "here is the answer." Science can't yet permit such bold and unsupported assertions. Instead, Ellis and Palmer would be well advised to be more careful in their writings. For example, replacing "this is why" with "our theory argues that."

Science is built upon the idea of skepticism. Pertaining to the Ellis & Palmer work, my skepticism leads me to several questions.

The available climate records during the Pleistocene suggest that the great maxima associated with each ice age have a duration of approximately 10,000 to 15,000 years. If the Gobi dust theory is indeed correct, why is the rebound onset so delayed? I recognize that Ellis and Palmer do argue that the delay in rebound relates to the arrival of a Milankovitch great summer. The definition of a Milankovitch great summer is quite broad. As the great summer spans over 5,000 years, it's hard to argue that the timing of the great summer arrival dictates the timing of Earth's temperature rebounds. I remain skeptical.

A second question concerns the manner in which the rebound out of the glacial maxima occurs. The available climate records make clear one point: The rebound and rapid temperature rise occur as a matter of discrete jumps or steps. Commonly these discrete steps are delayed, separated in time by approximately 500 years. An explanation regarding the discrete steps within the rebound period remains unanswered.

Nonetheless, I have considerable respect and appreciation for their work.

Ellis and Palmer's arguments concerning Gobi dust as a positive feedback that accelerates ice sheet melt are plausible. A key distinction between the Kleinian hypothesis and the Ellis & Palmer hypothesis is that Klein acknowledges that Gobi dust can contribute to increased ice melt but only after the initial onset of ice melt has occurred. In contrast, Ellis and Palmer argue that it is Gobi dust that initiates the ice melt.

• Ellis & Palmer's argument concerning the synchronization of Earth's temperature rebound with Milankovitch great summers retains plausibility but is not yet proven.

• Klein argues that the Ellis & Palmer hypothesis is hybrid, involving both positive feedback mechanisms and external drivers, described by Ellis and Palmer as modulation.

The Most Likely Answer

I HAVE ALREADY DISCREDITED astronomical and geological (external) drivers. The previous discussion acknowledges that the Ellis & Palmer hypothesis can conform or be in agreement with the Kleinian hypothesis. In addition, the merits of the Sergin & Sergin mathematical model likewise cannot be ruled out. The impact of orbital changes, broadly described as Milankovitch cycles, can also be at work simultaneously. In essence, one must consider that the four suggested hypotheses can coexist and be compatible, at least to some extent.

The situation of all four, or even more, mechanisms functioning simultaneously deserves consideration. Think, for example, of an orchestra or band playing. The musical group consists of a wide variety of instruments, such as woodwinds, strings, brass, and percussion. Although many groups have a conductor, the band can play despite the absence of a conductor. The question then arises: Which instrument or instruments function in setting the beat?

Although the answer can vary depending upon the piece being played and the instruments present, usually one group or instrument sets the rhythm, and that typically ends up being the percussion group, often the snare drums specifically.

Regarding climate, let us hypothesize that at least four distinct mechanisms are functioning simultaneously. Our four candidate methods are Milankovitch cycles, the Sergin & Sergin hypothesis, the Ellis & Palmer hypothesis, and the Kleinian hypothesis. Which one is setting the rhythm? Which of the four mechanisms is dominant and thus responsible for the 100K year cyclical behavior in the last 1M years? Absent the ability to conduct an experiment, we have few means available to arrive at a definitive answer. Nonetheless, I assert that one of the four theories is responsible for functioning as the pacemaker.

A quick note on Milankovitch cycles influencing glaciation causation: Remember that correlation does not equal causation. For example, ice cream sales and violent crime rates are closely correlated, but they are not causally linked with each other. Instead, hot temperatures, a third variable, affects both variables separately. In the same way, there may be a correlation between Milankovitch great summers and rebounds out of a glaciation, but correlation by itself does not prove causation.

Can You Prove It?

AS A CONTROL SYSTEMS THEORETICIAN, my underlying approach to problem-solving with modeling is to keep the model as simple as possible as long as the answers make sense and provide insight into the question. I will even claim that the greatest achievement for a control systems theoretician is to solve problems not by actually solving them, but instead by bounding the candidate solutions.

In this era where computers are king, one might ask if I have proved my hypothesis by a computer simulation or model. The answer, quite frankly, is no. The question buys into a false premise that the computer is capable of providing us with the desired answer. I have discussed the matter of simulation, weather predictions, and computer models in a previous chapter.

Clearly, unknowns still exist. Many facets need to be explored. Assuming somebody takes my hypothesis seriously, there will certainly be arguments concerning a multitude of how and why issues.

First, few people know much about what really goes on in oceans past the first 300 meters or so, especially if we are talking, for example, 14,000 years back in time. I believe that whatever might be going on down deep has little ability to alter what happens on or near the ocean's surface—except in the case of an ocean overturning. Naysayers are welcome to challenge my theory, but I doubt they'll be able to disprove it unless they are able to learn a vast amount more about what happens at great depths.

The role of compressibility of seawater based on pressure changes deserves discussion. Indeed, seawater becomes denser and thus compressible as hydrostatic pressures increase. The deeper the ocean, the higher the hydrostatic pressures, and therefore the denser the seawater. Although the change in density is modest, admittedly the density does change dependent upon the hydrostatic pressure.

In my discussion of the overturning physics, note that I have disregarded the compressibility characteristics of seawater. My reasoning is simple and justified. Bodies of water, such as oceans, commonly develop stratified layers of water. When a flipping is initiated based on density differentials, the role of compressibility is immaterial. Since flipping starts at a given depth, presumably at the interface of two stratified layers, one portion of the stratified layer might sink while an adjacent portion of the stratified interface rises. In essence, a rolling turnover is initiated between two portions of a common interface that share the same approximate depth. Thus, even though seawater density will vary with depth, the initiation of the rollover is a simultaneous action taking place at, or very close to, a defined horizontal layer. Even if deeper water is denser, it's not close enough to where the two strata of water meet to impact the initiation of turnover.

I am comfortable with a model that takes into account: (i) density (or the inverse, specific volume), (ii) water temperature, and (iii) partial pressures as related to the ability of the ocean to contain dissolved gases.

Several other questions face us in validating my theory. One challenge would be to sort through the Vostok ice core and related records with the goal of making sense of the higher frequency oscillations.

It's tempting to perform some sort of frequency or spectral analysis, perhaps using the Fourier Transform and digital software algorithms. Spectral analysis is a statistical technique for analyzing sequenced data by decomposing the sequence into oscillations of different lengths. The Fourier Transform is one type of spectral analysis, commonly used in heat transfer to convert the time domain to the frequency domain where linear operations can be performed and the results then converted back to the time domain. A spectral analysis study was by undertaken by Hodzic and Kennedy. I will not attempt to duplicate such efforts.

I have two concerns with spectral analysis:

1. The base cycle exhibits what I recognize as a jump. This makes me think of the Gibbs phenomenon, investigated by J. Willard Gibbs (1839-1903), which illustrates the folly of blindly applying Fourier analysis to a periodic signal with an abrupt jump or discontinuity. The problem, as Gibbs understood it, was that a finite series composed of smooth sinusoids is limited in its ability to represent discontinuous signals. A finite series approximation, thus a truncated infinite Fourier series, does not converge well and as

such will not fit the original signal well. In layman's terms, if your original time record has a jump, then even when you apply more terms to it, you're still going to see the same basic shape, and so applying Fourier analysis won't provide you any additional useful information. And this phenomenon may make the results of the analysis suspect.

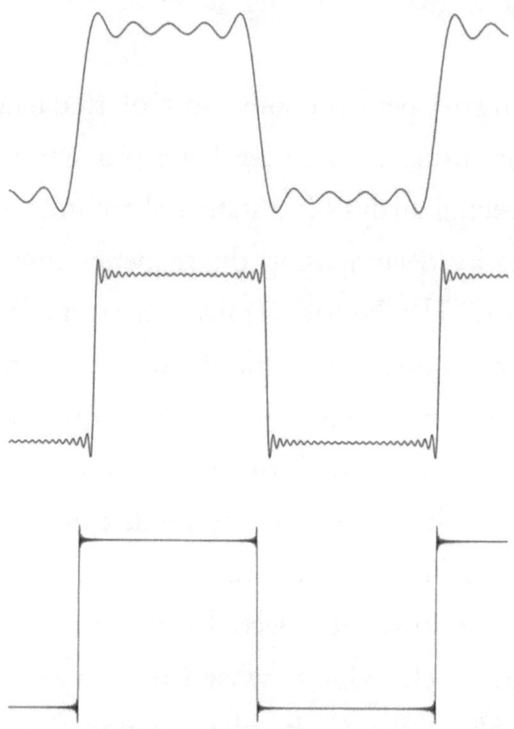

Fourier Series Functional Approximation of Square Wave using 5, 25, and 125 Harmonics

2. Earth's temperature record appears to be undergoing a slow downward slide. That descent is strikingly evident upon examination of the most recent 5.5M year history shown previously. The outcomes of any Fourier series analysis or approximation will

vary considerably depending on the choice of base time period, again making the results suspect.

Another challenge in validating the Kleinian Glacial Causation Hypothesis would be to delve deeper into the stability of the presumed 100K year limit cycle. Not all limit cycles in nature are stable. The fact that the Earth appears to have gone through as many as ten such cycles is insufficient for one to draw the conclusion that the 100K year cycles are stable. As a systems feedback theoretician, I'm sensitive to the possibility that our present climate system just might be unstable. If I observed a response in a machine or process similar to the 5.5M year temperature timeline above, I would become alarmed. When an oscillation emerges and appears to be growing in amplitude, or at least not decaying, that raises a red flag.

In the world that surrounds us, we seldom encounter unstable systems. Things that are unstable tend to solve (or even destroy) themselves. The question of the stability of the 41K year cycle in Regime Beta is moot. The 41K year cycle vanished and thus is only an historic topic to debate. On the other hand, the stability of the 100K year cycles in Regime Gamma deserves our utmost attention.

Currently, there is considerable alarm, even hysteria, over what mankind is doing that's possibly upsetting the climate apple cart. From a systems theoretic standpoint, whatever mankind does in the short term can potentially have a beneficial long-term effect, or conversely an adverse effect, or finally, little or no effect at all. At this juncture we simply do not have a sufficient understanding of the inherent governing mechanism of Earth's climate dynamics. In my considered opinion, it would be premature to jump to any conclusions.

What if We Did Know the Answer?

LET'S ASSUME that one could somehow validate my hypothesis, or any glacial causation hypothesis for that matter. What next? Assume for the sake of discussion that a climate truth, possibly even my hypothesis, is accepted. Assume next that we have enough knowledge, possibly through simulations, to permit us to conclude that in X years, Z will be the climate. Once that is known, the tendency is to jump to the next bright idea, such as, "We should push this lever Q to close window W and then pull string R and like magic, the climate forecast that we previously objected to can be tweaked to our liking."

But to your liking, my cousin Bob's, or mine? If an internal driver is identified as the climate culprit, I predict we will see enormous political fighting. If an external mechanism, such as an astronomical driver, is the cause, there will still be fights but perhaps less vicious. Mankind certainly has less potential to influence the universe if the Earth's climate machine is an externally driven system.

If mankind *could* influence the Earth's temperature, who should control the thermostat's setpoint? The only way a setpoint would work would be for the inhabitants of Earth to concede their individual freedom and render themselves subject to some all-knowing leader.

Of course, fossil fuel usage would be made illegal, but few would be content with having to place a pan of water in the sun to obtain hot water for bathing or laundry. There aren't enough rocks alongside open streams for all to wash their clothes. And it's a fantasy to think that the 8 billion inhabitants of planet Earth will all be in lockstep about adhering to a global climate regulation contract.

As for fine-tuning the weather, I prefer to let God be God and for us as humans to live under Him with what cards have been dealt to us. God has done marvels in His creation and in providing for us. Playing God would fail, just as the civil engineers in charge of the Tower of Babel failed.

On a historical note, I want to reflect on my childhood years following the close of World War II. The United States and other nations had fleets of surplus bombers. Plastic had become available. A proposal suggested using the surplus bombers to pull and then release large sheets of black plastic over the northern reaches of North America. The sheets would, in theory, lower the albedo by absorbing more solar radiation, and presto—portions of North America would become warmer. Man could then raise crops and live in areas that were previously too cold.

Do not underestimate the arrogance and stupidity of the human being, especially political types with grandiose utopian ideas.

Just as we can't obviate shivering and belching, we can't obviate the inevitable climate change cycle from repeating. Global warming advocates might insist on limiting carbon emissions or reducing the use of fossil fuels, much like a concerned parent might insist a child wear a coat if he's shivering or cover her mouth and say "Excuse me" if she belches. The point is, the Earth is likely to shiver again and the oceans are likely to belch again, and there's very little we can do about it.

Questions, Opinions, and Other Voices

"Never hear what I didn't say."
~Thomas Avery, Attorney at Law

I FIRST PUBLISHED *SHIVERING* IN 2020. Then I was invited to appear on a podcast (https://www.youtube.com/watch?v=l0bxbks2Izg). Following both, I have received numerous opinions and questions. I am addressing some here in a collage, along with my responses.

Bert Wald says: "We live in an age that will one day be seen as a time of over-optimism in science as a mechanism of government policy. The problem is that the model of science being employed is scientism, not science. Sadly, scientism has created perverse incentives such that The Science has acceptable and unacceptable theories and tests, and this creates a comfort zone that ruins proper science."

My reply: I agree wholeheartedly. I have stated numerous times that science indeed has limits. The questions of climate change and ice age causation are sufficiently complex that application of the scientific method leaves us empty-handed and scratching our heads. The scientific method is based on the adoption of four steps: formulation of a question or hypothesis, outlining a test whereby an experiment can be conducted, the acceptance or rejection of the hypothesis based on the experimental outcome, and the publication of one's findings along with sufficient information to permit an outside observer to replicate the experiment. We have but one Earth. We don't even own and thus control the environment of the entire planet, making it impossible to conduct an experiment. Moreover, even if we could conduct an experiment, Earth's reaction times are well beyond our human lifetimes.

In the absence of being able to apply the scientific method, an alternative is to engage in discussions, but our discussions are apt to fail because the questions posed cannot be proven using science.

Some literature suggests that water vapor is a greenhouse gas that causes warming, other literature such as Sergin & Sergin states that water vapor transitions through the cloud phase, therefore increasing Earth's albedo. When we discuss the role of water vapor in the atmosphere, it appears that two mechanisms are at work that are in opposition to each other. Because the goal is to model and thus understand the role of water vapor in the atmosphere, having two offsetting arguments is inconsistent. The unsettled nature of the matter demonstrates that theoretical models are little more than theory and certainly not established scientific facts you can bank on.

When I made the statement that water vapor acts as a greenhouse gas, I did so based on available commentaries in the literature [28]. I recognize that I cannot substantiate the accuracy of my assertion.

Our society has evolved into one where strong opinions abound. People of all stripes have adopted absolutist positions whereby they presume they have the answer. They don't.

Discovering the Garden of Eden says: "Why do atmospheres start cooling down sharply at the end of interglacials? Can a pressure decrease (i.e. due to heat or lots of water vapor being suspended) suddenly trigger a cooling?"

My reply: I have paraphrased the above question, but hopefully the intent has been preserved.

As the atmosphere cools, generally less water vapor will be present. Water vapor comprises approximately 0.4% of the mass of Earth's current atmosphere. Even if all water vapor were to be removed from the atmosphere, the surface atmospheric pressure would still be at 99% or more of the current. It does not make sense that cooling of the atmosphere causes sufficient atmospheric pressure drop, in turn causing an outgassing of the oceans. These dynamic actions may be occurring, but the feedbacks involved seem weak. Moreover, the suggested feedback mechanism constitutes a negative feedback—a cooling of Earth's atmosphere will not reinforce itself and thus bring additional cooling. Instead, the cooling of Earth's atmosphere will cause a reduction of water vapor and then of atmospheric pressure, thereby causing dissolved CO_2 to come out of the water, thus arguably causing an incremental *increase* in atmospheric temperature.

Keith Parker says: "How about a magnetic pole shift? Magnetic North changes place with the magnetic South, causing massive disruption."

My reply: The Earth hides its history and secrets well. It is generally understood that Earth's inner core is composed of molten iron, which is in turn surrounded by molten fluidic layers. Evidence abounds, such as in tree rings located in ancient bogs, indicating that the Earth has experienced prior magnetic pole shifts [29]. For example, researchers in New Zealand found evidence of Earth undergoing a magnetic pole shift approximately 43,000 years ago. The evidence of a magnetic shift in Earth's poles was also seen in solidified volcanic lava in Oregon [30]. As the magnetic poles might shift, life and weather patterns on Earth could be impacted. Because we have no evidence of cyclical magnetic pole reversals coinciding with the cyclical ice ages in the past 800K years, establishing any causal relationship would seem dubious. It's hard to resolve this question, but in short, I am not aware of any evidence to suggest a correlation between magnetic pole shifts and cyclical ice ages.

Max Tabmann says: "Before anyone can claim to have understood climate, he has to be able to explain the ice ages. Like Richard, I was never convinced that Milankovitch is the right explanation. Like Richard, I think it is not enough to explain the periodicity; one must also be able to explain the sawtooth-like shape of the temperature curve. The slow and almost linear descent into the cold may very well be caused by ice albedo feedback. This I would fully support. The rapid return to a warm period is a much harder puzzle and there I am skeptical about Richard's theory of rapid outgassing. I would favor another theory. During the cooling phase, enormous amounts of ice get attached to the poles. We speak of three kilometer (about two miles) thick ice layers there. This amount of ice changes the weight distribution of Earth and may cause a short change of its axis, which brings the ice into warm regions and thus instantaneously increases the amount of fluid water. This seems to be a much stronger feedback mechanism."

My reply: We certainly don't lack theoretical explanations about the climate! As Max's question attests, the role of mass redistribution is being considered. Yes, as Earth cools it is likely that ice buildup will occur on both poles. We know that the current Antarctic continent coincides with the South Pole. The current North Pole coincides with the Arctic Ocean. Ice buildup on the sea surface will not cause a mass concentration on that pole. Nonetheless, we need to consider both the Antarctica continent as well as ice buildup on the landmasses surrounding the current Arctic Ocean. I'll repeat: The Earth hides its history and secrets well. Yet ice core drillings, such as in Greenland, at Vostok, and at the EPICA center, suggest that the ice located in polar regions has been in place during the last Pleistocene epoch (the last 800,000 years). I am not aware of evidence of a change in Earth's spin axis, and thus its poles, occurring in the last 800K years. Therefore, the question remains open.

An order of magnitude comparison provides insight. The total mass of the Earth is estimated to be 5.97×10^{12} gigatons. The estimate for the current ice mass resting on Antarctica is 2.4×10^{7} gigatons. During a glacial maxima, the ice buildup resting on land will be greater than the current ice mass resting on Antarctica. Even a conservative estimate of, say, a tripling of the mass of ice resting on land will not materially impact the wide differential in ice mass compared to the mass of the Earth in its entirety. The ratio between Antarctica ice and the total mass of the earth differs by an excess of five orders of magnitude. This is akin to the comparison between a penny and an ice skater. The ice skater's dynamics will not materially change depending upon having or not having a penny in a pocket. The movement of ice toward or away from the poles lacks any plausibility in suggesting that Earth's spin axis can be influenced, and as such, I see little to no merit in Max's hypothetical argument.

Max's comment suggests that my theory explaining Earth's rapid temperature rebound is rooted in an oceanic degassing mechanism. That's not actually what my theory proposes. Yes, when bodies of water undergo density inversions and thus flip, some degassing commonly occurs. However, even if degassing of oceans would occur, other mechanisms can be at work to increase Earth's atmospheric temperatures. Available records suggest that temperatures rise first, with CO_2 increases lagging. The fact that temperatures rise *prior* to CO_2 increases strongly argues that a temperature increasing mechanism other than degassing is at work. I argue that changes in albedo constitute the primary mechanism behind temperature rises. Moreover, I theorize that as the oceans become unstable and thus flip, this disruptive action attacks sheets of sea ice. Wave action can, theoretically, cause floating sea ice to break and dislodge. Floating sea ice can thus change its position and drift to lower latitudes, where it can be further destructed as it reaches warmer waters.

James Arathoon says: "The land bridge between Russia and Alaska may have led to a sudden inrush of cold fresh water into the Pacific Ocean when it was broken during the exit from the last ice age."

My reply: It is my assumption that the Arctic Ocean remained connected to the North Atlantic over the time period being discussed. Even if a land bridge existed between Alaska and Eastern Siberia, the level of the Arctic Ocean would have remained in conformity with the North Atlantic. Yes, sea ice most likely covered all or most of the Arctic Ocean, but keep in mind that sea ice floats. The hydrostatic pressure within the Arctic Ocean would not be affected by the presence of sea ice. Consequently, I see no reason to conclude or even suspect that water or sea ice escaping over the land bridge had any significant contribution to the causation of the rebound out of the last glacial maxima.

Dave Cummins says: "To say the climate cycles are definitely not driven by external forces is surely shaky. That is, as the Earth moves within the solar system and the wider galactic systems, external gravitational forces must impact on the Earth's geological structures and therefore influence plate tectonics and hence volcanic activity. Perhaps not the only force but certainly one of them? Just a thought."

My reply: Dave's points deserve merit. Recall that I speak in the language of mathematics and the related mathematical models intended to describe the behavior of physical systems. Dynamically speaking, a movement or change within a process can be caused by external forcing and/or internal stability issues, or even what are called time-varying systems. Dave suggests that orbital mechanics can alter gravitational forces, thereby leading to plate movements and volcanic action. Indeed, the movement of plates and the onset of volcanoes possess the ability to alter Earth's climate. In these instances, the causal origins of climate changes would be classified as externally driven because climate itself has little to do with orbit mechanics behaviors.

Internal and external mechanisms can be at work simultaneously to impact Earth's climate and cause ice ages. For example, an external mechanism would be changes in Earth's orbit, with Milankovitch cycles as a prime example. One cannot argue that Earth's inbound radiation isn't impacted by variations in Earth's orbital mechanics. However, while Milankovitch cycles may be present, other forces or dynamics internal to Earth's weather machine can also be at work. For example, as Earth's atmosphere warms, such as in a rebound out of a glacial maxima, it is understood that seawater will degas, thereby causing an increase in atmospheric CO_2. In turn, the increase in atmospheric CO_2 will cause an increase in the greenhouse effect, causing an additional increase in Earth's atmospheric temperature.

So, some external mechanisms can be at play, and both internal and external mechanisms can be at work simultaneously, but I wouldn't give the external mechanisms too much credit for their role in driving the climate cycles. As I've mentioned before, if some astronomical driver were at play, it would have to consistently occur every 100K years, or the new cycle would have to continue on its own in this new pattern without any further intervention. I find this highly improbable.

Al White says: "I suppose Mr. Klein is unaware of the perfect correlation between the Milankovitch cycles (specifically eccentricity and precession) which dramatically change the level of solar radiation (the Earth's only meaningful source of heat) reaching the Earth, and the 100K year glacial cycles. Before you propose any alternate driver of climate variation other than that you would first have to prove that a large change in energy input would not have an effect on climate. Mr. Klein's idea that the climate system is completely internally driven is silly."

My reply: Mr. White starts his remarks asserting that a perfect correlation exists between the Milankovitch cycles and the 100K year glacial cycles. I assert that no record of Milankovitch cycles exists beyond what the sediment layers and ice core drillings reveal. If one uses sediment and ice records to define Milankovitch cycles, then obviously Earth's periodic glaciations will perfectly match up with the sedimentary and ice records—the coincidence occurs because a circular argument was invoked.

As for the amount of solar insolation "reaching" Earth, I disagree with his use of the word "reaching" since the same amount of energy arrives on Earth from the sun, regardless of the Milankovitch cycles. If he meant to discuss the net quantity "reaching" the Earth, i.e. factoring in reflected energy, then it is true that Milankovitch cycles could affect it, but that is not normally implied in the use of the word reaching.

Note also that the glacial cycles of approximately 100K years in the Pleistocene do not always coincide with Milankovitch cycle dynamics. It's true that based on Ellis and Palmer's documentation, the glacial rebounds during the recent Pleistocene have coincided with what they describe as Milankovitch great summers. However, the glacial rebounds are not in rhythm with all Milankovitch great summers. As such, I have reservations regarding the sacredness of Milankovitch cycles and their role in orchestration of ice ages.

Some researchers have suggested that Earth's inbound solar insolation can vary up to 25% as dictated by Milankovitch arguments. I acknowledge that eccentricity can alter inbound insolation, but only by about 3%. However, I reject arguments asserting that precession impacts Earth's inbound radiation by up to 25%. Precession can alter Earth's spin axis but has imperceptible impact on the distance between the sun and the Earth. Absent additional information, such as the orientation of landmasses relative to Earth's orbit plane about the sun, claims that solar inbound insolation is significantly altered appear to be meritless.

Milankovitch cycles stem from orbital variations such as eccentricity being impacted by gravitational poles from large planets, like Saturn and Jupiter. Saturn, Jupiter, and Earth have been orbiting the Sun for considerable durations, certainly well prior to the onset of the recent Pleistocene. If Milankovitch cycles indeed cause dramatic changes in Earth's inbound radiation, we should see some evidence of cyclical variations in Earth's climate prior to the onset of the Pleistocene. But instead, Earth's climate record prior to 3 million years ago has no cyclical correlation to theorized Milankovitch cycles. Again, in my mind, the absence of pre-Pleistocene cyclical dynamics timed to Milankovitch cycles affirms that the causation of Earth's ice ages in the last 800K years has its origins in internally driven feedback mechanisms.

To conclude, we are engaged in an intellectual debate. All participants should be welcomed. Questions raised by commentators must be viewed positively. In each of the cases above, I have enjoyed providing responses.

I have previously commented that the hysteria surrounding climate change has placed people at odds with each other. Such visceral disdain for others with opposing views is tragic. Opposing opinions should be welcomed, because when two views vary, the opportunity for advancing truth is at hand. I relish the opportunity to dissect a complex logic chain. The ability to examine two or more seemingly contradictory theories allows for fertile ground in the quest for truth.

I wish all those who commented the best in life's journey.

SCIENCE

"In the cold, shivering twilight, preceding the daybreak of civilization, the dominating emotion of man was fear."
~ Paul Harris

Scientific Illiteracy in Today's Society

EVERYONE ENGAGED IN THE CLIMATE CHANGE DEBATE has a right to their opinion, even those less familiar with technological concepts. But I also have the right to dismiss the opinions of those I deem to be technically illiterate.

Climate alarmists claim that science is on their side, but reality tells a different story. Climate alarmists tend to know little about science and even less about heat and energy. Not only are so-called climate experts lacking in scientific knowledge, but the general public is as well. Science involves immersion in a culture with specific rules of conduct—and many aren't playing by those rules. Here are but a few examples.

In an article, a source attributed to NASA states that as Earth's tilt or obliquity changes, the maximum tilt angle is 24.5 degrees and the minimum tilt angle is 22.1 degrees [31]. NASA has provided each of these bounds to three significant digits. I argue that nobody from NASA has ever observed and recorded those two extremes. Instead, some theory, not definitively spelled out in the NASA post, was used to permit a calculation. Humans have limited records concerning changes in Earth's tilt angle. The ancient Babylonians, about 5,000 years back, noted that Earth's rotational axis pointed to a different star, that is, different than Polaris. Having such records is helpful, however much more is needed to explain with precision a mechanism for the ongoing changes in Earth's obliquity. As a presumption, the calculation of Earth's maximum and minimum tilt angles was based upon a two-step process: (i) theorize a mathematical model of obliquity changes, and (ii) assume physical parameters as required for the model. The Earth has a molten core, which also clouds the picture. In short, it is a gross disregard for science for an institution like NASA to publish tilt angle extremes implying accuracy of three significant digits. It is indeed sad that junk science so permeates our culture and governmental agencies that no one even noticed the absurd statements.

An older example entails the history of Mount Everest. Mount Everest was named after Sir George Everest because in the 1850s a surveying team in India was commissioned to determine the height of the greatest peak in the Himalayan mountain range. The objective was to use triangulation based on surveying techniques to ascertain the height of the presumably tallest mountain in the world. The triangulation computations yielded a result of 29,000 feet. The expeditionary team was befuddled. The expenditure for that trip was immense. To give the simple answer of 29,000 feet would not be acceptable, so the expeditionary team changed the number to 29,002 feet. Having a fifth digit of accuracy satisfied the political scheme, justifying the massive cost. Incidentally, the measurement was later revised to 29,032 feet using more accurate methods.

The rules of science are inviolate. A scientific thinker should never state any numerical value to a precision that is not in accord with the facts. But in our society, we believe whatever we are told, provided the proclamation includes three significant digits along with a decimal point.

Yet another example is in words with Latin roots. The word centrifugal is based on the idea of the fugitive fleeting from the center, and it refers to the apparent force exerted on an object that pushes it outward from the center of a circle. Interestingly, many believe that centrifugal forces exist in nature. This is an absurdity. A centrifugal force may appear to be present, but its appearance stems from an improper usage of Newtonian mechanics. Newton's laws of motion are valid only in an inertial coordinate system. If Newton's laws are improperly applied to a non-inertial coordinate system, that leads to a faulty conclusion. In order for a coordinate system to be inertial, it must be non-accelerating. When most people refer to centrifugal force, they are referring to a rotating reference space which is accelerating and therefore non-inertial, and are most likely confusing the term with "centripetal force." Centripetal forces do exist in nature, whereas centrifugal forces do not. Centripetal force is what keeps an object moving in a circular path, such as a planet orbiting the sun.

But that's not the only instance of improper language usage in science. The words "data" and "datum" are, respectively, plural and singular. Sadly, many who claim to be scientists flunk the most basic of grammar tests. We commonly hear so-called scientists declaring "the data shows that…" but because "data" is plural, the correct statement should be "the data show that…" The incorrect usage is so common today that few can even spot it.

Still another example is with the concept of wind chill as proclaimed by the media. Wind chill cools warm things down more rapidly, but it doesn't make the object colder than ambient dry bulb temperature. Once an automobile, for example, has been parked outside overnight, the ability for that vehicle's engine to start is not impacted by wind chill. After a car's engine assumes ambient temperature, cold is cold. In short, wind velocity has no bearing on the temperature of cold metal that has been left outside a sufficient duration. When I gave my students a quiz some years ago, 80 percent of supposedly educated engineering students had been duped into thinking that wind chill somehow made an unheated object colder than ambient.

I haven't run out of examples yet. In my college days, some 65 years ago, mathematics and engineering students used a device called a slide rule to perform calculations. Slide rules function based on the concept of logarithms. As such, multiplication is a process whereby logarithms are added and subtracted. Although the slide rule could commonly yield answers to three significant digits, it didn't provide for the placement of the decimal point. The student therefore needed to augment the calculation process by estimating orders of magnitude. The placement of the decimal point was determined based on some quick mental gymnastics. With the introduction of the electronic calculator and now the smartphone and all its variations, the public has no need to perform such mental exercises. The generations that followed me have scant ability to perform calculations mentally. Even store clerks handling money each day can't think. Their predictable response is to reach for a smartphone or other electronic calculating device and start keying in numbers. Our population at large is emotionally involved in climate hysteria, yet they can't even estimate orders of magnitude.

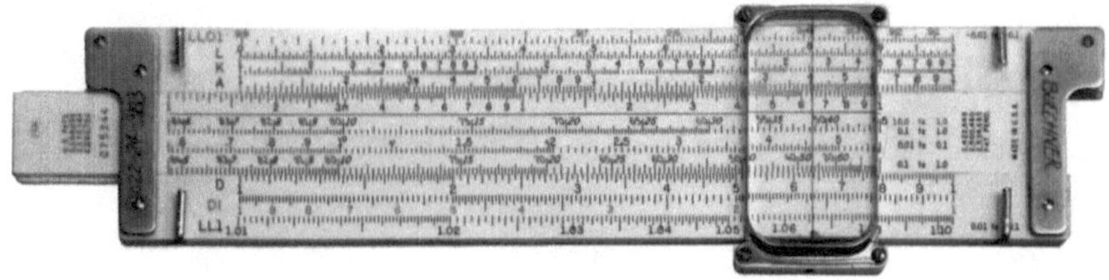

Slide Rule

The integrity of scientific thinking even among supposed scientists has suffered. Complex problems such as explaining the causation of periodic glaciations will not be resolved so long as we allow our deficiencies in scientific thinking to perpetuate—through laziness, through reliance on the media, and especially reliance on lazy scientific thinking shared through the media.

Deficiencies in Mathematics Education

WE COULD BE MUCH FURTHER ALONG in resolving the climate dynamics problem if we had better instruction in mathematics.

Relatively few people are familiar with feedback systems methodology—only a small percentage are even exposed to feedback systems principles and methodologies. Much of the reason for this stems from mathematics professors. Mathematics courses as taught in the typical large university curricula are dictated by tradition. Perhaps the archetypal course is Ordinary Differential Equations, abbreviated as ODE and also as DEQ.

In order to understand how DEQ is taught, it helps to understand the role of mathematics departments in the educational culture. The vast majority of students taking math courses are not math majors. Math is taught as a service to engineering students, accountancy majors, biologists, meteorologists, and such. Math professors disdain such teaching assignments of the "unwashed" masses of non-math majors, but the math department budget depends on the service courses such as calculus, DEQ, or statistics, provided to the larger student population.

Students are forced to take math courses; math professors are forced to teach them. No one is happy, except for the holy few math majors who also get to take the rare higher-level math courses.

The DEQ course serves as a filter to weed out weak or unmotivated students before they get into the heart of the engineering curricula. Some "bust out" courses perform this service well, typically culling half the students.

The subject matter taught in DEQ was obsolete a century ago, but nobody seems to care. Solving a differential equation means that somebody has somehow managed to find an analytical expression (also known as a solution) that bounds the differential equation as well as any stated initial or boundary conditions.

Not all differential equations have solutions that can be expressed in closed form, meaning built upon elementary functions. Common elementary functions include polynomials, trigonometric expressions like sine and cosine, and exponentials. The universe of possible functions is immense, and the few known elementary functions make up only a small part of that universe. It's absurd to suggest that all or even most differential equations have solutions expressible as some combination of elementary functions. There are many classes of functions beyond the known elementary functions, but these are few and far between. Examples of higher order functions include the Bessel function, the Gamma function, and the Gauss error function. It is appalling that mathematics instructors commonly fail to state the paucity of functions expressible based on elementary functions.

Mathematics instructors believe in certain foundational concepts, two of them being existence and uniqueness. Because mathematics and the solution-finding process are often tied to arguments based on existence and uniqueness, this creates a rabbit and the hat situation. When mathematics instructors are faced with solving a DEQ, they usually know the answer in advance. They will then tell their students to assume a solution. The instructor proceeds to demonstrate that the solution—the rabbit plucked out of the hat—satisfies both existence and uniqueness. Of course, it is vastly easier to pose a problem if one already knows the answer. This is a part of the landscape in how mathematics is presented. This method of teaching denies the student an audit trail, thus denying the student of the inner thinking in determining how to pluck a certain rabbit out of a certain hat. Although mathematics instructors delight in pulling rabbits out of hats, the student is left bewildered and helpless, not having gained any discernable insight in how the solution was assumed. One thing is abundantly clear: The vast majority of students enrolled in DEQ detest taking the course.

In the teaching of DEQ, the equations are not linear in most cases. Methods do exist for finding solutions to linear time-invariant equations, but these methods aren't mainstreamed. Instead, the focus is on finding solutions to nonlinear and/or time variable parameter equations. Since the Renaissance, only a handful of nonlinear differential equations have been solved analytically, meaning in closed-form.

Few people in today's world want to solve differential equations in closed-form. In those cases when a numerical solution might be desired, digital computing techniques are available to crunch out solutions.

When students undertake the study of calculus, they easily master the elements of differentiating, but find the task of performing its counterpart—integrations—to be an immense hurdle. I call this situation the paradox of calculus based on one fundamental argument. If we abandon analytical notations but instead focus on building physical devices, we quickly discover that one can't build devices that differentiate, but rather we can easily build devices that can perform integrations. Differentiation is a noise amplifying process. As a result, any physical device attempting to perform a differentiation lacks the ability to display successive derivatives. In contrast, integration is an accumulation and thus a smoothing process. It is vastly easier to be able to construct and operate devices that integrate given input signals. Most instructors of calculus, being focused on analytical manipulations, grossly fail to point out this paradox.

My conclusion, based on my career in teaching systems theoretic principles, is that there are three types of people: (i) those who never studied calculus, (ii) those who studied calculus but only achieved a rudimentary grasp whereby most facts where memorized—and they've since forgotten what they learned, and (iii) those who understood calculus in its fuller meaning. People in the relatively rare third grouping understood that integration was straightforward and relatively easy, whereas differentiation being incorporated into devices was formidable and, in a theoretical sense, not achievable.

So why do students have to take a course in DEQ? And why

hasn't DEQ been brought into the 21st century? Little to no effort has been expended to make DEQ relevant in today's world.

This reminds me of the phrase in economics called "opportunity cost." Whenever one undertakes an activity, the decision to engage in that activity implies that other activities were excluded. This is where opportunity costs come into play. I submit that two costs are involved in DEQ education. The first is the opportunity cost, specifically because the student never ventured into an alternative pursuit. The second is that the pedagogical teaching method of DEQ developed thought processes that yielded negative returns. In essence, exposure to DEQ as traditionally taught resulted in inefficient and non–yielding problem-solving approaches.

What is lacking and yet desperately needed is for feedback systems theoretic methods to be taught as a replacement for traditional DEQ instruction. Unfortunately, the likelihood of this happening is nil. Mathematics departments have scant motivation to even attempt a change. The only places within university curricula for teaching systems theoretic principles is within the engineering realms, such as in electrical, chemical, and mechanical engineering. However, the faculty in most of those departments have little motivation to teach systems theoretic principles, as the majority of those professors prefer their own specializations and subject areas.

Yet another hurdle to any improvements to the DEQ curriculum concerns accreditation. The accreditation of engineering programs in the United States is the purview of the Accreditation Board of Engineering and Technology, Inc. (ABET). Higher educational institutions are highly traditional and jealously protect their accreditation. Any attempt to nudge DEQ out of a curriculum, thus replacing it with some uncharted substitute, has zero chance of being blessed with ABET's approval.

You may be asking: Why hasn't Richard Klein authored a text for a substitute course for DEQ?

Good question! I did try during my tenure at the University of Illinois, but my proposal didn't pass the committee review board. A consistent trait of mine is that I have always been at odds with and at the losing end in committee deliberations, and this was no different. Some of the faculty members on the committee viewed the teaching of Control Systems as an extension of DEQ, with an emphasis on manipulation of complex algebraic symbols and arduous, time-consuming daily homework assignments. Others on the committee were well-spoken foreign nationals whose air of competence surpassed their actual knowledge of the subject matter. Not to mention many of these people were thermodynamicists, with little more than a basic understanding of feedback systems methodology. Because of their collective opposition to my ideas and pedagogical approaches, I was unable to bring in a new wave of thinking for our math students.

A second reason I never authored a book on the topic relates to the poor economic returns associated with book authorship. When I was actively teaching, the total number of mechanical engineering graduates annually in the U.S. was about 10,000. At that time, I would be lucky to achieve sales of 1,000 books annually—and that's only for new books as no royalties are earned on resales. Even if one writes a successful book, it's hard to capture more than 20% of the market. Unless you're in a broader genre, like microbiology, in which my brother Donald saw success with his textbook since there are 300,000 students annually, there's just not enough volume.

Yet another reality is that textbooks become dated and obsolete. Most smaller schools desperately fight to maintain their accreditation, and as such will reject any text that is five years beyond its original publishing date.

The economics just aren't there.

To top things off, our Dean of Engineering looked down at any professor who spent time authoring books. Instead, the Dean rewarded faculty members who received large research grants and published scholarly articles in high-ranking peer reviewed journals.

So, it is with sadness that I reflect on having never authored a book on how DEQ should and could be replaced with a book founded on feedback systems principles. Maybe we would be in a better place today to discuss the climate change problem.

The Six Tiers of Educational Taxonomy

A NUMBER OF EDUCATIONAL RESEARCHERS have delved into the question of "educational goals." Notable among these is the work of Benjamin S. Bloom in his *Taxonomy of Educational Objectives*, which summarizes the work of a national committee and forum of prominent educators [32]. It's important to note that the word "educator" is not in reference to one who purports to educate, but rather one who has studied the educational process itself.

Most higher-level educators, including engineering professors, may consider themselves educators, but have only a scant knowledge and understanding of the "educational" process itself. Educators are, with very few exceptions, professionals who have specialized in a field and then instruct others in their thought processes. The thought processes of the specialists are almost exclusively that of deductive reasoning, based upon some given or taught first principles. For example, engineering professors, for the large part, view their teaching obligation as the task of presenting foundation principles, and then of providing examples as to how those principles may be applied to a spectrum of carefully selected examples.

Bloom, in marked contrast, concludes that education in creative problem solving is a six-level hierarchical process, of which knowledge and its direct applications are only the first level in his taxonomy. Before one can advance to a higher level, mastery at the prior levels must be achieved. The six tiers are, starting at the base level:

Memorization

Understanding facts

Ability to apply facts

Analysis

Synthesis

Evaluation

It is fair to say that the vast majority of educational focus in current academia is on the base levels, related to facts and understanding of facts. Critical thinking and effective problem-solving attain their pinnacle as the upper levels of Bloom's taxonomy are reached. During my teaching career I strived to stimulate students and introduce them to the upper levels of his taxonomy. As an odd twist, I found that challenging students to think quickly at the upper levels tends to create discomfort. Memorizers prefer to memorize; critical thinking is avoided. I encourage those interested in education to learn more about Bloom's taxonomy.

As it pertains to understanding climate dynamics, the opportunity to apply evaluation—Bloom's sixth hierarchical level—must be reached.

Deficiencies in Computing and Simulations

OUR ABILITY TO SOLVE THE CLIMATE PROBLEM hinges on one's mathematical maturity. A solid grounding in mathematics and associated computing techniques is necessary. Although the digital computer with its high processing speed and an abundance of memory is available, the computer itself doesn't shout out "this is what you need to do." Computers require programming. The computer can't do a thing until a command is given, which requires strong thinking skills to attack differential equation solution problems.

In contrast, an alternative form of computing, the electronic differential analyzer, beckons the user. These types of computers are commonly referred to as analogue computers. The heart of the analogue computer is the usage of high gain negative feedback amplifiers. High gain negative amplifiers are able to analogue, or model, mathematical operations, notably being able to integrate an input or a signal in real time. (I am using the word integrate in the mathematical sense, as it relates to differential and integral calculus.)

Integral Sign

As a historical note, the operational amplifier was developed based on the work of Harold Black at Bell Telephone Labs in New Jersey in 1927. To some, his invention is considered the most important breakthrough of the twentieth century in the field of electronics, as it has a wide area of application. An unfortunate reality is that a negative feedback amplifier can be unstable such that it may oscillate.

Upon recognizing that a high-gain feedback amplifier could at times become unstable, the electrical engineers and mathematicians at Bell Labs pursued a remedy to circumvent the problem. The solution came in the form of an experimental finding by Heinrich Bode. Bode observed that a feedback amplifier would be stable provided the open-loop frequency response had certain characteristics. Bode's conclusion was that the slope of the log-log plot as it crossed the horizontal axis was subject to constraints. Subsequently, Bode's empirical findings were replaced by the 1932 analytical findings of Dr. Harold Nyquist. The Nyquist stability criterion can now be found in many textbooks on feedback control theory.

Once the stability problem had been solved, the negative feedback amplifier became extremely useful in the field of electronics. Black published a famous paper, Stabilized feedback amplifiers, in 1934 [33].

Analogue Computer

Analogue computing technology was strongly influenced by the computing needs required to win **WWII**. The first practical analogue computer of the war era, based on the work of Dr. Vannevar Bush, was developed at the Massachusetts Institute of Technology and incorporated mechanical devices and not electronic equivalents. Specifically, the ball and disk integrator was a mechanical device that could integrate a variable, hence a signal, in real time. This device incorporated six ball and disk integrators, thus permitting differential equations up to sixths order to be solved.

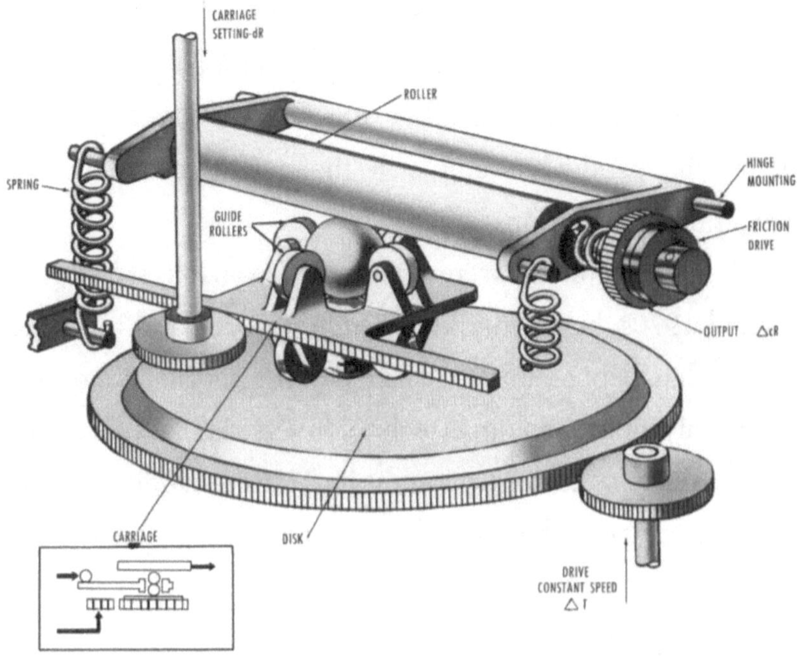

Ball and Disk Integrator

Analogue computers continued to evolve in the post-WWII era, switching from a focus on mechanical devices to electrical devices. The strength of an analogue computer rests in its ability to perform simultaneous operations. The heart of each operation is an operational amplifier, but analogue computers can be constructed to permit simultaneous operation of many such operational amplifiers. Because DC voltages can be manipulated by usage of nonlinear components, analogue computers can address and solve problems containing nonlinearities. Typical components that can be useful in solving nonlinear problems include diodes, voltage-multiplying devices, and programmable nonlinear functional relationships.

So, analogue computers can be programmed—or perhaps the

better word would be "patched"—to perform multiple simultaneous operations. One prepares the machine's operational amplifiers to be interconnected by wires. Each is subject to DC voltage changes whereby the patched circuit will then analogue some desired outcomes, hence solutions.

Analogue computers were commonly available starting in the 1960s and 1970s, but to my knowledge, the demand for analogue computers has all but vanished. Note that the Sergin & Sergin work relied heavily upon analogue technology as their work coincided with the heyday of analogue computing. Understanding the Sergin & Sergin work would be easier if today's researchers had the mindset of an analogue computer programmer.

The analogue computer could be controlled to perform high speed repetitive operations. The output could be displayed on an oscilloscope. The speed of the calculation could be adjusted by merely changing the magnitudes of all capacitances. While the machine was in repetitive operation, the user was free to tweak a potentiometer knob, thereby changing a gain within the patched circuit. It was sort of a game to cause the shape of the computed response to change by continuously observing the oscilloscope's output shape as the potentiometer gain knob was increased or decreased. In a sense, the experienced programmer could seek out how the programmed mathematical model responded to a myriad of "what if" questions. Having a programmed, or patched up, problem became an instructive and delightful rapid pursuit.

Analogue computers came with drawbacks, including high maintenance costs, inability to achieve high accuracy, and lack of documentation. The lack of documentation concerned both the patch cord configuration as well as the inability to store output responses, notably in tabular form. I am sure that programming packages are available whereby modern digital computers can mimic analogue computers, but in my mind, the pursuit isn't the same.

When considering use of digital computers to simulate climate conditions, keep in mind that simulation is not a proof. That statement, made by K. Poolla of UC Berkeley, is vitally important, so I will repeat it. ***Simulation is not a proof.*** One needs to be highly skeptical of any "scientist" who claims to have created a computer model that simulates the Earth's climate machine.

The reality is that no computer program can accurately replicate the dynamics of the Earth's weather machine. Weather has been shown to be chaotic, meaning that small variations can lead to vastly different outcomes. A second reality is that the climate system is incredibly large. The dynamics are indeed dynamic. A computer simulation needs initial conditions. The computer simulation then needs to replicate the advance of time. Those who advocate using computers to validate the future know little about computers and simulation.

No computer could ever hope to embrace the Earth's complex climate dynamics. Yes, computer models can be created, but first one has to lump the motion and behavior of near countless molecules into a finite number of discrete entities so as to cause the order (the dimensionality) of the model to be workable. The rub comes because the outcome will depend on the assumptions about an immense system when we lack an understanding as to which variables are important and which can be discarded or at least lumped.

Weather prediction even a week away is an inexact undertaking at best. Any computer model claiming the ability to predict worldwide climate years ahead should be viewed as alchemy or sorcery.

Moreover, a skilled programmer—and I once upon a time possibly fell into that category—can come up with endless numbers of models that will predict whatever it is that I or the programmer might wish the outcome to be.

Modeling Deficiencies

EARTH AND ITS CLIMATE MACHINE don't afford the opportunity to conduct a scientific experiment of any hypothesis. No computer model exists or can be written to replicate Earth's climate machine on the scale required. Even if a scientific experiment could be conducted, we don't have the luxury of waiting 90,000 years to observe an outcome. We can't give Earth a double-blind study by testing a population of representative Earths.

In certain cases of scientific pursuit, scale model testing has provided insights. Wind tunnels have been used to allow aerodynamicists to study the mechanics involving aerodynamic drag and wing foil lift, for example. Scale models can also be used to study how tall buildings react aerodynamically to movement of air in Earth's boundary layer—the buildings can be represented by models with heights of approximately one meter that will, in theory, tell aerodynamicists how a building over 300 meters in height will behave when subject to wind loading. Scale models can also help determine the drag on a ship's hull.

Scale model testing is not practical if one wants to study and predict glaciation causation. All scale model testing relies upon the application of the Buckingham π Theorem. This theorem stipulates that natural phenomenon will behave independent of the choice of units for scale measurement. An equation can be rewritten in terms of a set of dimensionless parameters constructed from the original variables, but in the case of climate modeling, the variables are unknown. The dynamics of Earth's climate system are vastly too complex and nonlinear to ever permit the construction and study of a scale model of Earth. In short, the concept of using scale models to replicate and thus study ice age causation is not a viable option.

Therefore, like Einstein, my arguments are based on inductive reasoning and are limited to application of mathematics combined with reasoning.

Insolation Misconceptions

ANOTHER EXAMPLE OF DUBIOUS THINKING in today's scientific atmosphere is assertions made regarding magnitude changes in Earth's insolation—the inbound solar radiation—due to changes in obliquity and precession. Precession is defined as the motion of the axis of a spinning body, sometimes just called "wobble."

I argue that variations in Earth's insolation are not strongly influenced by obliquity or precession. Obliquity refers to the angle of tilt of the Earth as it spins on an axis relative to the orbital plane. The Earth might be free to change its tilt angle, but these variations don't greatly impact the quantity of insolation the Earth receives. My reasoning is simple. As the Earth orbits the sun, the Earth remains spherical. Some slight bulging might be present, such as that caused by gravitational pulls from nearby heavenly bodies, but the Earth's shape is largely spherical. As a sphere, the only factor influencing the quantity of inbound solar radiation is the distance between the Earth and the sun. I submit that although the Earth might tilt and wobble as defined by its spin axis, the tilt and precession do not alter Earth's distance from the sun.

The quantity of insolation received by Earth does vary according to the distance maintained between the sun and Earth, but obliquity impacts only the seasonal effects. Said in other terms, as Earth's tilt increases, this will lead to greater seasonal variations. Independent of Earth's tilt, the level of insolation received does not vary, because the seasonal highs and lows will average each other out.

Of course, while inbound solar radiation is impacting Earth, the amount of reflected radiant energy due to albedo can vary. Albedo refers to the fraction of sunlight that is diffusely reflected by a body or planet. The strength of the albedo is dependent upon the positioning and orientation of landmasses as the Earth spins on its axis. I assert that any discussion of how Earth's radiation balance does or does not change is meritless if one lacks specifics regarding the distribution of landmasses vs. open seas relative to Earth's spin axis. Calculations of changes in Earth's radiation balance are absurd unless additional parameter values are known. Notable parameters are Earth's temperature wherein ice sheets are subject to variations and a time history of Earth's spin axis relative to its geological features.

To explain why obliquity and precession of the Earth in its orbit have little effect on inbound solar radiation, I like to use the analogy of hog roasting. If a hog is on a spit over a fire, the net heat from the fire to the hog is largely independent of how the hog might be rotated on the spit. Yes, if the rotation rate is low, or even zero, then the pig being roasted might burn on one side and be undercooked on the opposite side. In the case of Earth orbiting the Sun, the Earth is undergoing spin while it orbits in its annual path around the Sun. The relatively high spin rate gives us a large number of days and nights during its annual journey.

The Fallacy of Milankovitch Cycles

Some people in the climatology community argue that orbital changes, commonly known as Milankovitch cycles, can significantly alter Earth's insolation. For example, Alan Buis states in an article that "these cyclical orbital movements, which became known as the Milankovitch cycles, cause variations of up to 25% in the amount of incoming insolation at Earth's mid-latitudes (the areas of our planet located between about 30° and 60° north and south of the equator) [31]."

We have scant evidence to support claims that obliquity and precession somehow contribute to changes in our inbound solar insolation. Obliquity and precession relate to the tilt angle and wobble of the earth, but in no way impact how much solar insolation strikes the planet. On the other hand, eccentricity of orbit will influence the distance between the earth and the sun.

Deeper within this question one should ask, how were

Milankovitch cycles first calculated? Few humans were on Earth, say, 600,000 years ago. We have no definitive proof or evidence of when Milankovitch cycles did or did not occur. Instead, the Earth has passed down to us a climate record in the form of sedimentary deposits and ice buildups acquired through sedimentary records and ice core drillings. In the period between 1911 and 1941 when Milankovitch published his findings, he explored the question of periodic ice ages based on examination of sedimentary layers. Yes, it is reasonable to conclude that Earth's orbit mechanics involve three modifications—eccentricity changes, obliquity (tilt) variations, and precession (wobble). The laws of orbital mechanics based on Newtonian physics are well understood. Unfortunately, application of these laws requires assumptions regarding simple things like Earth's core being solid, or conversely, Earth's core being molten. Humans have yet to know precisely what is going on within Earth's molten core.

To complicate matters, the molten core of the Earth is mostly composed of iron. Iron has magnetic properties, as attested to by Earth's magnetic north and south poles. We have some evidence showing that Earth's magnetic poles have shifted and even possibly reversed over time. The magnetic fields that would have caused such changes or reversals as Earth orbits the sun are not fully understood at present. One thing does seem clear: If a magnetic field external to the Earth somehow alters its molten core, this implies movements.

What Earth's shell or mantle might be doing is yet another unknown. My point is that as we study Earth's behavior and climate history, we have far more questions than we have answers.

Of course we can make simple assumptions, but one can get

entirely different answers regarding calculations of Earth's dynamics depending upon what assumptions are made. One way of circumventing this problem is to use an evidential record that provides a time history of Earth's orbital behavior. So it seems that a circular argument has been invoked. Based on some climate record, notably ice cores or sediment layers in rock, one can adjust the parameters within an orbital mechanics model so that the model will precisely replicate the geological and/or ice record. The next sleight of hand is to say that now we know the orbital cycles history, or the Milankovitch cycles, and the perfect coincidence of the Milankovitch cycles with the record constitutes proof of the causality of glacial dynamics. But of course the two records will agree, because the initial determination of the Milankovitch cycles was based upon precision in curve matching to the climate record.

CLOSING

"Life is like a blanket too short. You pull it up and your toes rebel, you yank it down and shivers meander about your shoulder; but cheerful folks manage to draw their knees up and pass a very comfortable night."
~ Howard Marion-Crawford

Answering the Climate Change Question

At the outset of this climate discussion, I promised to answer the question of climate change. Yes, the Earth's climate is changing and has been changing for all recorded time. The climate won't somehow magically settle down, and especially to a temperature and condition of our choosing. Mankind failed in the story of the Tower of Babel. Similarly, we have scant ability to change Earth's future temperature.

Mankind's puzzlement with ice age causation and the subsequent search for answers based on science remain unfulfilled. Absent the ability to apply the scientific method whereby experiments can be conducted, humans are left with little other than intellectual debating. I have put forth my hypothesis arguing that the recent ice ages are rooted in internal dynamics and thus feedbacks. Perhaps my greatest contributions to the current climate debate are: (i) that climate dynamics are internally generated within the earth's sphere; and (ii) the "why" question concerning ice ages will require adeptness with feedback systems theoretic principles.

During the late Pleistocene, the ice core records, notably the EPICA, show that the successive rebounds out of the respective glacial maxima periods occurred as discrete and abrupt warming events. For example, during the rebound out of the last ice age, the Wisconsin, the rebound was characterized by three abrupt jumps. Here is a question for those who support arguments based on Milankovitch cycles: Can Milankovitch cycle theory suggest mechanisms causing the rebounds out of glacial maxima periods to be discrete and step-like?

I assert that Milankovitch-based solar variations are gentle and certainly not abrupt. In contrast, my hypothesis that the ice ages are based on internal mechanisms, notably limit cycles, holds promise in this regard. I theorize that ocean dynamics are involved. Oceans and bodies of water can be stable for long periods of time, and yet at times, bodies of water can undergo abrupt changes. I hypothesize that during a glacial maxima period, sheets of sea ice cover ocean surfaces in higher latitudes. Commensurate with a density inversion, it is theorized that a body of water will overturn. I thus argue that a dramatic event such as an ocean overturning will lead to shattering of portions of ice sheets and accelerated sea ice melting. Note also that should sea ice sheets ever fracture, the sea ice is capable of movement into areas of warmer water, but the drift or movement of the fractured portion is subject to some restraints. Obviously, the fractured portion would be blocked from drifting to a higher latitude region because non-fractured ice sheets are presumably in place. A segment of fractured ice sheet, assuming it can drift, has little alternative other than movement to lower latitudes. I argue that such shattering of sheets of sea ice would, in the end, result in abrupt decreases in Earth's albedo. I argue that this theory conforms to the observed abruptness in Earth's temperature rebounds out of ice ages.

Powerful positive feedback mechanisms are presently in charge of the Earth's climate balance. The good news is that Earth is enjoying a brief respite from cold as we are in the midst of an interglacial period. The bad news is that history shows that interglacials end and are followed by glacials. I am confident, short of an intervention by God, that in the next 90,000 years the Earth will descend into another ice age. We as humans are but tiny specks flowing along in a river called time.

The positive feedbacks responsible for Earth's climate are orders of magnitude more powerful than any minor rearrangement of the deck chairs on the *Titanic.* Also, the timescale is controlled by dynamics over which mankind has no power.

Consider, for example, the ice mass resting on Antarctica. The block of ice is typically several kilometers in depth. The air temperature is well below the freezing point. When viewed as a lumped mass, the ice present has a time constant measured in the order of thousands of human lifetimes placed in sequence. Any suggestion that mankind can melt that ice, say, in a human lifetime, is preposterous. Yes, some melting is taking place, but the melting is deep, concentrated at the underbelly where the ice is resting on the landmass.

And yes, mankind is releasing some carbon gases into the atmosphere. Yet carbon gases are constantly being exchanged between the atmosphere and oceans. The oceans contain vastly more carbon gases than the atmosphere, with about 38,000 gigatons in the ocean compared to about 3,200 gigatons in the air. The distribution of carbon dioxide is also in constant flux, as carbon can be absorbed by plant and animal life as well as ocean water and rock sediments.

Large population concentrations on Earth don't share in the present hysteria over release of carbon gases. China has a population in excess of a billion people. India's population rivals China's. To add to this, the population of the African continent falls just short of one and a half billion. It is folly to think that all of mankind will agree to go back to living in the stone age based upon some misguided climate hypothesis formulated by pseudo-experts with scant grasp of the climate record and virtually no grounding in systems theoretic principles.

During my years as a professor at the University of Illinois, the circumstances of my academic duties mandated that I not venture into such high-risk areas of research as glacial causation. Furthermore, I needed to focus most of my time on being a productive faculty member, and my teaching load was significant.

But at this point in my life, I am in my golden years. Three things now combine to work in my favor: (i) I am retired so I have more free time, (ii) the climate record is becoming increasingly clearer as more findings are published, (iii) and now that I'm not a tenured faculty member, I am able to take previously unthinkable risks. I am having a wonderful time and enjoying every minute.

Winston Spencer Churchill stands as perhaps one of the most influential persons of the 20th century, although he was not always in public favor. During the 1930s, he was a minority member of the British House of Commons. He gave fiery orations in the House of

Commons, but at his home, in order to relieve his frustration, he laid bricks to build a brick wall. Visitors would observe Churchill and comment on his wall. The wall wasn't straight. The mortar wasn't uniform in thickness. The rows of bricks weren't level.

Winston Churchill Laying Bricks [34]

Criticism was the common theme. Nobody observing Churchill laying bricks would acknowledge that his brick wall was indeed perfectly functional. Despite its imperfections, the wall could do everything that a brick wall should do.

I have similarly labored to lay my bricks. My bricks have outlined a glacial causation hypothesis. I expect that the critics of my hypothesis will be abundant. To each of them I have five things to say:

1. Show me your own glacial causation hypothesis.

2. The Kleinian Glacial Causation Hypothesis indeed stands, just as Churchill's brick wall stood and I presume still stands.

3. I submit that the Kleinian Glacial Causation Hypothesis is compatible with all available Earth climate records.

4. I assert that the Kleinian Glacial Causation Hypothesis satisfactorily passes all five proposed screening tests as annumerated previously.

5. I invite critics to explain where my hypothesis is flawed.

When I tell people I authored a book on climate change, I am commonly asked if I can shed light. Can I provide basic facts to help them counter the hysteria? They are hoping for clarity in what has become a muddled debate. They crave something solid that will allow them to form an opinion. Some grasp that Earth has recently come out of an ice age but most don't realize that Earth has experienced multiple periodic ice ages.

Here's a summary of a few foundational considerations:

- The melting of sea ice has no impact on ocean levels.

- Oceans behave differently depending upon the degree to which stirring occurs. Some recipes call for occasional stirring, yet other recipes call for a non-stirred cooking time. The outcomes are strongly influenced by stirring or the absence thereof. The same holds true for oceans as participants in Earth's climate machine.

- Earth's radiation balance has strong positive feedback mechanisms, the strongest being albedo.

- Other positive feedbacks exist. Atmospheric dust will cool the Earth, thereby leading to colder and more arid conditions—and even more airborne dust. The colder atmosphere with more dust feeds on itself.

- Pointing a finger at mankind as the sole contributor to global temperature changes is flawed science and flawed logic.

- Likewise, blaming mankind for causing ocean levels to change is ludicrous. Climate is dynamic. Ocean levels have deviated in excess of a hundred meters from present levels—in both ways. No causal proof exists tying any changes to mankind's presence.

- Should the Earth's atmospheric temperature incrementally increase, that increase will not cause a significant increase in melting of land-based ice. This point is critical in understanding Earth's climate.

Let me elaborate on the last consideration as it may seem counterintuitive. The majority of ice resting on land mass is in Antarctica. Antarctica is a desert. The atmosphere is so cold that it holds very little water vapor. The ambient air temperature is well below freezing, reported to be typically -43 degrees Celsius.

If the air temperature increased, say by three degrees C, that rise would be insufficient to cause an increase in ice melt. However, the rise in temperature would cause an increase in precipitation. Snowfall in Antarctica ultimately would cause an increase in net ice accumulation.

The Antarctica ice cap is subject to some melting. Most melting takes place on the underside of the ice cap, not on the air-to-surface interface. There is very little snowfall. Moreover, most snowfall remains and adds to the ice buildup. Based on the Vostok core record, 3,600 meters of ice resulted from 420K years of accumulation. The average annual buildup is, roughly speaking, a mere 1 centimeter per year. We observe that virtually no melting or loss of ice took place at the surface. If upper ice melt had occurred, the Vostok core record would have a missing time block. The Vostok record, instead, is continuous from present day and goes back without a break to 420K YBP. In addition, the published findings of EPICA provide a continuous record going back 800K years. Again, the melting of Antarctica ice takes place, in large, at the interface between ice and land.

Antarctic Ice

According to Sergin & Sergin [23], the Antarctica continent has been in the throes of ice now going on 20 million years. Because Antarctica is predominantly ice-covered, the surface area remains constant. Yes, some changes in thickness take place over time, but

Sergin & Sergin assert that for the last one million years the volume of ice resting on Antarctica has varied very little, exceeding +/- 7%.

The activities of mankind are incapable of causing ice to melt thousands of meters down under an ice coverage that has been in place for a million years or more. The response of the Antarctica ice cap cannot be altered in the brief timeframe associated with the presence of mankind.

It all boils down to orders of magnitude. The glacial causation mechanism exists. With or without the impact of mankind, the far greater threat to our present life and well-being is the next glaciation. Mankind has lived in cities for the past 10,000 years at most. Anybody seriously concerned about what the climate will be in 90,000 years is living in a fantasy world.

Because a small increase in air temperature has the opposite effect of what most people expect, it seems illogical. It acts counter to our simple human logic and thinking. In a sense, climate shares attributes with bicycles. Bicycles are strongly counterintuitive. If you wish to turn right, you should first initiate the turn by turning left.

In addressing the climate change hysteria, let's take the same approach. Rather than turning in the same direction as the unfounded alarmists, let's head in the other direction—toward logic and reasoning.

Politics or Science?

MANY OF THE PLAYERS engaged in the current climate debate are out of their league. They are either uninformed, or they are outright charlatans deliberately out to deceive us. Or both.

The climate causation question is immense. Politicians and social activists have inserted themselves into the debate. They have assigned life and death importance to what is right and wrong in deciding our societal actions.

In a sense, the hysteria over climate change is akin to a doomsday proclamation. I've encountered numerous doomsday predictions and warnings in my life. In the 1950s, society was in dread fear of contracting polio. I recall in 1959 being able to go water-skiing on a lake with no other boats and with empty beaches. The public was too scared that summer to venture out for fear of contracting polio.

As a consequence of the threat posed by the bomb in the 1950s, building fallout shelters in homes became popular. School children were trained in drills to hide under their desks in their classrooms. Banks offered long-term financing, typically a 30-year mortgage, for fallout shelter construction. That is, until they realized the inconsistency of financing end-of-life shelters for 30 years.

In the mid-1970s we were told that we would all freeze because of the pending ice age. We were told that Earth's ability to sustain humans was limited to about 5 billion people. Scarcity of food would bring widespread starvation. Yet Earth's current population is about 8 billion persons, and food doesn't seem to be an issue. Of course, climate alarmists now tell us that we will all perish, and soon, due to global warming. Doomsday scenarios have always been with us.

Mechanical engineers believe in the doomsday end of life because they consider the Second Law of Thermodynamics to be the bedrock of the universe.

This fundamental tenet of the mechanical engineering profession states that, when the universe is considered as a closed system, it will approach a constant temperature. Absent temperature differentials, there can be no useful work attained from cyclical heat-powered engines, as all things approach a common temperature, so thermodynamicists assert. Heat-powered engines require a colder sink in which to discharge energy. That explains why power plants are commonly placed adjacent to rivers and other large bodies of water. Absent available water sinks, an alternative is the cooling tower. In any event, engines based on thermal cycles require a place in which to discharge heat.

Mechanical engineers consider the Second Law of Thermodynamics sacrosanct. To them, it is everything. No life or activity of any kind will be possible due to this predicted lack of available energy. Of course, no time scale is provided by the doomsday prognosticating thermodynamicists. Quite frankly, the universe seems to have been doing well for the last 13.7 billion years, so I presume that the end of life will occur on some time scale measured in billions of years.

The rest of the world doesn't share the view of mechanical engineers. Stars will continue to exist. Life will go on. I appreciate the insights provided by Second Law, but I still sleep pretty well each night.

As the climate debate rages in our society, it is all too common that farming practices are being called into question as a prelude to doomsday. It is presumed that farming is responsible for adding CO_2 to the atmosphere, thereby bringing our certain demise, notably by drowning. My wife's brother and his family operate a sizable dairy farm in eastern Iowa. Brother Jack (not his real name) farms about 2,000 acres and has a dairy herd milked by robots. I asked Jack about his views concerning the morality of farming. Jack commented:

"Farming yields, say, with regard to corn production, have tripled in the last half century. In 1970, a corn yield of 100 bushels per acre was considered good. Now, with improvements of genetics and application of technology, corn yields have increased to 300 bushels per acre."

This dramatic increase in yields makes one point clear: Farmers like Jack continue to meet world demand for food. Recall that even in my lifetime, cries went out saying that the planet was at its limit in providing food if the world population ever reached 5 billion.

Companies involved in chemical production, seed genetics, and agricultural machinery have steadfastly brought about innovations. As one example, the John Deere brand now offers a product called See and Spray®. The spraying device traverses the agricultural land, selectively applying herbicides. Cameras and digital logic aboard the sprayer unit recognize weeds and spray herbicides to just those weeds. The corn and soybean plants are passed over. The reduction of chemicals used is significant. Yields have sharply risen. Meanwhile, the adverse impacts on the environment are minimized.

Improvements in cropping technology continue. The days of the moldboard plow are a distant memory. No-till farming has become the standard. The number of times the farmer must traverse the ground with equipment has been reduced.

Genetic improvements to plants, under the descriptive label GMO (genetically modified organisms), have permitted production yield improvements, along with resistance to adverse factors such as insects and drought, and the ability to grow in colder climates.

It is frequently argued that cows adversely impact Earth's climate because they pass methane. Numerous studies, including some in peer-reviewed journals, argue otherwise. When the entirety of the carbon cycle is taken into account, dairy cows have a neutral carbon impact on the climate. Cows consume legumes and thus intake carbon in their diets. As ruminants, cows will pass methane gases. Chemically speaking, methane breaks down in the atmosphere as the methane molecules revert to the more stable forms of CO_2 and H_4. The suggestion that cows need to be banned is based on hysteria and not on any actual fact. Over the span of a decade, the time required for methane to break down, the dairy cow can be said to be carbon neutral.

Climate change alarmists are even seeking to ban pizza. A primary ingredient in pizza is cheese. Cheese is made from milk. Milk comes from cows. Methane is argued to be a greenhouse gas pollutant, thus a contributor to global warming. Cows are alleged to pass gas, notably methane. The end game is clear: Pizza must be banned, otherwise we will all die in 2031.

Getting rid of cows means that pizza will become a thing of the past, like buggy whips, whale oil for lamps, and knickers. Personally, I look forward to any attempt to outlaw pizza. The effort will result in most pizza lovers exiling the climate change alarmists to a distant island in Lake Vostok in Antarctica. Down there they can live pizza-free, far away from the ravages of global warming.

To Save the World, We Must Ban Pizza

Climate alarmists are determined to make social change at all costs. As evidence of this, the state of New York recently legislated that gas stoves and gas heating will no longer be allowed in commercial buildings exceeding seven stories. Activists elsewhere are at work to outlaw stove ranges that use gas. The state of California has mandated that small internal combustion engines, such as for lawn mowing and leaf blowing, be prohibited. California is even enacting laws restricting goat herds. Interestingly, goat herds eat foliage and can push back fire hazards. Although claiming fires are caused by global warming, alarmists argue for the elimination of goats. California is also implementing legislation whereby diesel-powered trucks will be outlawed. Everything is being done because urgency demands. We must stop using fossil fuels, otherwise we will all perish!

As for me, I plan to cook a pizza in my gas oven tonight and might even enjoy a bowl of cereal with milk tomorrow.

Humans Pretending to Be God

*"Be fruitful and multiply and fill the earth and subdue it,
and have dominion over the fish of the sea and over the
birds of the heavens and over every living thing that
moves on the earth." - Genesis 1:28 (ESV)*

A FOCAL POINT IN THE DEBATE over climate change regards the morality of using fossil fuels. Climate alarmists spread fears as they proclaim that doomsday is at hand, while some accept the gift of fossil fuels and steadfastly use these resources to better the lives of Earth's inhabitants. Similarly, mankind debates whether it is moral or immoral to irreversibly impact the planet.

Two schools of thought as extremes emerge. One theme is that the Earth deserves to be allowed to carry on in a pristine manner, thus implying that mankind should depopulate the Earth. Few people have come up with meaningful ways to depopulate the Earth, but certainly all 8 billion inhabitants drinking Kool-Aid of the Jonestown variety would suffice. The second school of thought is that God and his vision clearly commanded mankind to be fruitful and to multiply. The debate between the two is unlikely to come to a mutually acceptable resolution. My goal is to bring logical thinking and mathematical rigor to the debate.

Am I alarmed at the thought of humans digging up fossil fuels? In answering that question, I am reminded of a phrase spoken by Pastor Malcom Nygren, now passed on, of Champaign, Illinois. Pastor Nygren remarked, "The gift was meant to be opened." Nygren was referring to the settling of the vast heartland of the United States. With the coming of migrant settlers from the extreme corners of the Earth to the American continent, the abundant resources of America's heartland became available to support this nation and its many peoples.

Some lament the destruction of the pristine prairie and its life. I submit that even the indigenous peoples living in this continent have benefitted immensely from the opening of the gift. They are now more populous, have better lifestyles, and would never want to go back to the living conditions of their forefathers. Although many might decry how the indigenous peoples are oppressed, these claims don't hold water. All people living in this vast nation today are immersed in a society that is blessed with opulence and untold opportunity. All persons desiring to improve their lot are free to make their moves. Education is available to all. We live in a world where knowledge is virtually unbounded, one only has to reach out and grasp for it. Indeed, I stand firm in my belief that the gift was meant to be opened.

The current struggle over climate change boils down to the

matter of humans pretending to be God. Climate alarmists, to a large extent, deny God as creator and instead look at themselves as the ultimate adjudicators. Yet in the passage from Genesis 1:28, scripture makes it clear that God, as creator, proclaims his vision for mankind and the Earth. My view is that God is God and that we, as humans, have been commanded to be his people, subject to his authority.

Why has the doomsday crowd selected climate change as their hill to die on? Certainly, similar arguments could have been applied to other facets of human activity.

My belief is that the climate alarmism seen today is a selective argument with one specific goal in mind: The progressive factions within our society are seeking control. The issue at hand is not climate change, global warming, and melting ice where we will all drown in 12 years. It's interesting to me that climate alarmists, and virtually all alarmists, select a time period that appears imminent, but is still slightly out of reach. Doomsday predictions that life will end tomorrow aren't taken seriously. Doomsday predictions that all life will end in billions of years, such as those expressed by advocates of the second law of thermodynamics, likewise aren't taken seriously. But rather the goal is for the progressive elements to take over society. Make no mistake, the supposed concern over climate change is a ruse. The objective is undeniable. The objective is to win the next several elections.

Do I worry about global warming? My answer is a firm negative. I put my faith in God and His plans, which go well beyond the next election cycle.

What's Next, Doc?

I've enjoyed the chance to share my climate trek spanning the past half century. It's timely to pause at this point to take stock, reflect, and ponder "What's next?"

For most people, following the global warming debate is merely a spectator sport. The issues are complex, requiring special skills and training if one hopes to actively participate. For the majority, it's tempting to sit on the sidelines like Spock and use words like fascinating and interesting. These words don't involve risks. Risk-taking can be left to other combatants. But at some point, this writing will likely attract the attention of those with vested interests.

As climate change is a polarizing subject, there will be scant middle ground. Those who have strong opinions will gravitate to one extreme or the other. Some will consider my thoughts as a prayer answered—like manna from heaven. Yet others will find them as repulsive as the stench traveling downwind from the belch of a hog waste lagoon.

A lone piece of circumstantial evidence, such as might be presented in a criminal court of law, will seldom sway a jury's verdict. But it all changes if the jury is presented with four, eight, or more pieces of circumstantial evidence.

Here is my vision for the future validation potential of the Kleinian Glacial Causation Hypothesis.

My hypothesis has ventured into a vastly uncharted territory. I have staked out flags—landmarks. The nature of the hunt now changes dramatically. Researchers have guideposts. They will know where to look and what to look for. Similar to the rising slope of the curve in the familiar scientific S-Curve, new findings will come relatively easily. Only modest efforts will be required to achieve significant results. The search for truth is akin to walking into a lush orchard with plentiful low-hanging fruit.

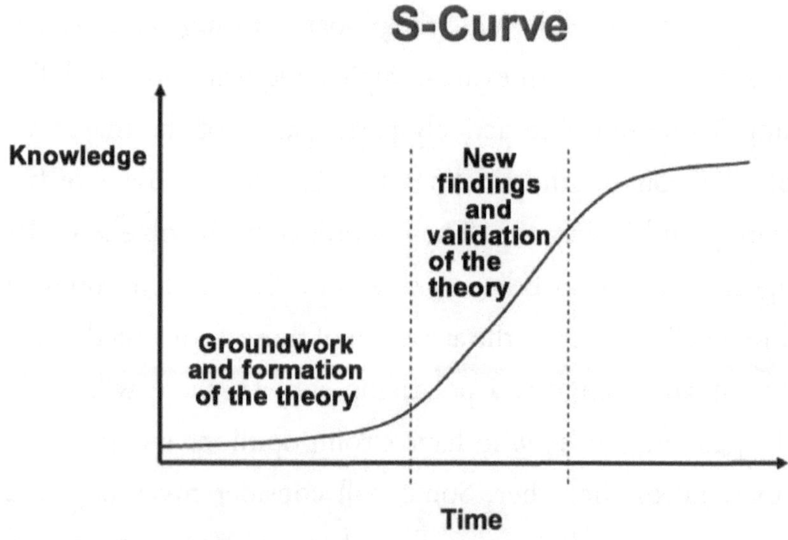

S-Curve of Knowledge Vs. Time

Just for discussion purposes, grant me the assumption that the Kleinian Glacial Causation Hypothesis indeed represents a landmark entry into such a bountiful setting. Others coming after me will find new pieces of the climate puzzle and put those pieces into place. At some point, assuming my hypothesis is valid, a sufficient number of circumstantial findings will fall into place. Conversely, if my hypothesis is invalid, its lack of validity will become apparent. However, if the future puzzle pieces support my hypothesis, the jury will shift its verdict in my favor. If a favorable verdict is reached, this will not truly reflect science, but instead opinion.

As newly validated puzzle pieces continue to support my hypothesis, a politicization process will begin. Politics will weigh in. An interesting aspect of the Kleinian Glacial Causation Hypothesis is that its focus is on climate dynamics being local to the Earth. Once the local nature is generally accepted, whether true or not, politicians will have enormous power and advantage. The skeptics and climate alarmists will turn on a dime to embrace any theory supporting the need for humans to be in charge.

I have paid my dues and have put in my time. The baton is being handed over to a new generation of runners in the race, to compete in the marathon. When and if the day ever comes, I will rejoice in being proven wrong. Because I view the glass as half full, I am optimistic that my ideas will bear fruit.

The world is engaged in an enormous struggle over seeking an answer to the question: Is mankind upsetting the climate apple cart? Is mankind marching off a cliff, about to drown like countless suicide-crazed lemmings? Hysteria and panic abound. My unique position is that like the canopy of the banyan tree, I can see downward to understand numerous nuances and details. While hordes are screaming and running about like chickens with their heads cut off. I am at rest and at ease. I have an abundant grasp of the broad climate picture. And I have a plentiful stock of coats and scarves for the impending ice age.

APPENDIX A: THE ORIGINS OF THE GRAND CANYON

REFLECTING ON MY TREK for the past half-century it's clear that, as noted by Neil Armstrong, rocks shout out truth.

In discussing my Kleinian Glacial Causation Hypothesis, other longstanding geological mysteries become relevant. One such mystery concerns the origins of the Grand Canyon.

The evidence indicates that the Grand Canyon was cut into layers of rock by recent flood-related events. The Colorado River now follows the canyon's path, but the myth of grains of sand eroding away the rock over hundreds of millions of years is absurd. The evidence is abundant and openly visible: the rock as it was cut and the virtual absence of cut rock at the exit. As a geological event, the Grand Canyon is freshly cut. If the erosion took place over hundreds of millions of years, freezing and thawing would have smoothed the outcroppings. The pronounced V-shape of the cut suggests a sudden and strong cut. Hundreds of cubic kilometers of rock were removed and washed away, and yet no alluvial buildups of sand exist downstream.

There are no similar canyons anywhere on Earth.

I reason that the most recent ten ice ages resulted in ocean overturnings, each then causing enormous tidal waves. Being the first to suggest such giant ocean waves, I have proclaimed them as Kleinian Waves. These waves repeatedly filled the Great Basin in the western part of the United States to the point of overflowing with sea water, debris, and ice. Once some of the surface rock was cut away, a path for water to flow to the sea was established, thus cutting deeper and deeper.

The Grand Canyon

I also conjecture that substantial chunks of ice were carried along with the water's surge. The ice came from a combination of two sources: (i) sea ice carried along from the Pacific Ocean by a giant wave, and (ii) glacial ice sheets already in the Great Basin. Geological evidence shows that the forces to initiate the cut must necessarily have required more than liquid water. The upper levels of rock were hard, whereas under the upper hard crust the softer sandstone was vastly easier to erode.

This mass of water and ice operated in a giant grinding action. The removed rock was quickly flushed to sea. Slow moving waters, in contrast, deposit sediments. The cycles of filling and emptying of the Great Basin cut the Grand Canyon. Each of the ten recent ice ages and subsequent ocean flipping and degassing had the potential to contribute. Also, each climate rebound most likely caused multiple Kleinian Waves. As an illustration, we know from geological evidence that the most recent Wisconsin ice age rebound came in three abrupt warmings. The repeated actions took place within the last one million years, considered recent in geological terms. Once a path to the sea was cut and available as a drain, the present Colorado River followed that path.

All geological evidence supports such a Grand Canyon carving scenario. An example of another flooding, also supported by geological evidence, is the Missoula River in Northern Idaho, which was flooded to a depth of approximately 640 meters [35]. The enormous rush of water at that time exceeded the flow of all present rivers on Earth combined. The Missoula flood and its great onrush of water have led to numerous theories. One theory is that the waters making up the Missoula basin were held in place by an ice formation or dam. Please note that the Kleinian ocean overturning hypothesis suggests an alternative explanation for the sourcing of the Missoula flood waters.

Another datum point comes from the Great Salt Flats in Utah, also referred to as the Bonneville Flats. Most geologists accept that the salt flats resulted from residues of salt in water that evaporated. But how was it possible for so much salt to come just from rivers? I see a connection. The successive Kleinian Waves caused the Great

Basin to fill repeatedly with ocean water, water with significant salt content. But why didn't other basins, such as the Dead Sea basin, also fill? I conjecture that the Great Basin saw more sea water invasion because of its proximity to the Pacific Ocean.

I will leave it to scientists not yet born to work out the computer model simulations.

APPENDIX B: GENESIS AND THE GREAT FLOOD

I MUST CONFESS that I had so much fun writing about my theory that it was hard to stop. It's sort of like eating peanuts. At this point I assume the reader understands the Kleinian Glacial Causation Hypothesis. Note I said "understand" which isn't necessarily being in agreement. Agreement is the reader's choice but is not a prerequisite for reading on. An extra-credit objective is to ask whether my hypothesis is compatible with the Genesis account of the great flood (Genesis 6-9). I find virtually complete compatibility. Please bear with me and enjoy.

The Biblical account of the great flood at the time of Noah is worthy of a fresh reading. Biblical truths in the Genesis account are, in my opinion, abundant. It's difficult to read the Biblical account of the great flood and not be dazzled by the many on-target insights of the ancient writer.

Here are just some examples:

- Based on the Genesis account (cf. Genesis 2:5-6; 7:4, 12), it appears possible that rain did not happen until the time of the great flood. This correlates to the fact that in the midst of an ice age, atmospheric relative humidity would be extremely low. Arid conditions would prevail. There would be no significant precipitation.

- Once the flood came, torrents of rain poured down (Genesis 7:4, 11-12). In periods of low relative humidity, the air retains much dust, i.e. fine particulate matter. Note that the Vostok ice core affirms that high concentrations of particulates were present during glacial extremes. Raindrop formation is a critical mechanism in keeping the atmosphere relatively free of dust particles. But the prior period of prolonged low humidity meant that rain had not been cleansing the air, and the atmosphere had become heavily laden with minute dust particles. The sudden increase in atmospheric water vapor following an overturning of deep ocean water, with its accompanying gas release or belch, would make conditions ripe for copious precipitation. The released water molecules, now in vaporous form, had abundant dust particles with which to start the precipitation process. Thus, a deluge of rain came down.

- During the great flood, not only did it rain in torrents, the waters from beneath gushed upward (Genesis 7:11). The *English Standard Version* states that the fountains from deep were turned on. When a deep body of water overturns, it feeds on itself. As bubbles form and rise, a stirring mechanism is created. The surface level rises dramatically as the bubbles expand on their upward surge. The overturning body of water, in this case the ocean, develops a frothy head, just as carbonated beverages develop foamy heads. Large volumes of toxic gases are released. Woe be to all creatures that have nostrils. Foamy bubbles will not buoy the swimmer up sufficiently to breathe fresh air. Even a strong swimmer or someone clinging to, say, an uprooted tree, would be asphyxiated and perish. And remember that the overturning also generates massive Kleinian Waves, drowning anyone who hasn't already asphyxiated. Skeptics discount the Genesis flood story, citing that Earth lacked adequate water to reach to the mountain tops. But the image of waters rising and then receding after 40 days of rain is a western invention. I see no basis to view the deluge as a quasi-static event. Drowning and asphyxiation would rule the day, or even the minute.

Noah's Ark

- If there's one place to possibly ride out the deluge, it would be in an enclosed ark. When the ocean overturns—belches— it releases large quantities of carbon dioxide and methane, gases that in the short term would hang as low-lying gas clouds, displacing the normal mix of oxygen and nitrogen in the atmosphere. It stands to reason that when dissolved gases are released from ocean depths, they're concentrated and thus would be capable of snuffing out life of any breathing creatures. In theory, nostril-breathers could remain inside the ark, at least until the gas cloud had mixed with adequate amounts of air to dilute the poisons.

- God commanded Noah and his family to construct the ark.

- God specifically instructed Noah to include a hatch in the ark that could be closed and sealed (Genesis 6:16). Note also that it was God, not Noah, who closed the hatch at the appropriate time (Genesis 7:16). The biblical account does not indicate the ark had sails, oars, or a rudder. Based on the progression of the narrative, the ark was designed by God for a single purpose: to preserve a remnant of living creatures while God's just judgment was poured out on violent humanity (Genesis 6:5-14). As a sealed and enclosed vessel, Noah's ark would float above the waters of destruction. While the biblical account does not draw attention to this fact, the pitched-sealed ark could also protect the creatures and Noah's family within from any toxic gases. The ark wasn't a tropical cruise ship. It was designed to simply float while remaining sealed.

- The account in Genesis goes on to say that winds came upon the Earth when God began concluding the flood (Genesis 8:1). After the overturning, the released gases would be colder and somewhat heavier than the surrounding air. Winds, due to the reestablishment of weather patterns, would cause atmospheric mixing, thus diluting over time the low hanging toxic gas clouds.

- Noah released a dove and it later returned (Genesis 8:8).

Canaries have been used historically in mines to warn the miners of bad breathing conditions below the surface. As long as the canary was well, all was well. When the canary died, that signaled the miners to exit. Such animals are called sentinels. Birds like doves and canaries have a faster breathing rate, smaller size, and higher metabolism compared to humans. In toxic air conditions, the sentinel bird would succumb before humans. When the dove returned to Noah, it was a sign that the outside air was safe to breathe.

- A rainbow appeared in the sky following the flood (Genesis 9:12-17). A rainbow will occur only when the atmosphere contains sufficient moisture, which would happen following an ocean overturning. It is possible the rainbow would have never appeared in pre-flood times as the atmosphere lacked adequate water vapor.

Central to the Genesis account, God gave the rainbow as a promise that He would not send another flood to "destroy all flesh" (Genesis 9:15). I find God's promise uplifting, but also a puzzlement. My engineering mind sees the prior pattern of ten periodic ice ages. God's promise of the rainbow assures me that He will not permit another ice age. Ice ages require extended periods of arid conditions. Upon extrapolation of the climate record of Regime Gamma, successive ice ages would seem to fit the pattern. I must accept that God has other plans in store. Scripture speaks of the Second Coming of Christ and the end times. I trust in the Lord. Even given the insights of my glacial causation hypothesis, I place my bets that mankind will never be successful in being a stabilizing thermostat on Planet Earth. Instead, I am content to leave it in God's hands.

The first five books of the Bible, and Genesis in particular, were most likely an oral history. The Book of Genesis is now thousands of years old. Our present-day knowledge of science and Earth's climate history became available only very recently. For example, Lyapunov's works were unknown in the West until after World War II. The Vostok record was published within the past four decades. Yet the Genesis narrative fits like a hand in a glove. The ancient accounts in Genesis conform in detail with cutting edge scientific findings.

Again, the account in Genesis is truly dazzling.
The Bible is a piece of literature. It is the inspired word of God, that being a foundational premise of Christians. In writing the Bible, God used many human hands and minds. Different writers adopted a wide variety of writing styles. Some Biblical books are poetry. Others are expository. The list could go on.

Ancient Hebrew is a playful language and its imagery is also bountiful. But then English (as an example of a western language) also uses pithy and picturesque imagery when the occasion is fitting: "Kill two birds with one stone," "a watched pot never boils," "long in the tooth," "don't bite the hand that feeds you," "don't put the cart before the horse," etc.

Since the Enlightenment, western people have frequently been what I would call uncooperative readers. Many have tried to read Biblical accounts like the creation or the flood accounts as if they were intended to be scientific accounts. In contrast, good readers cooperate with the writer's communicative purposes. I will cite a modern example. It is uncharitable to attack someone for saying they waited forever in a check-out line as if the speaker's point was to be precise with time. Of course they didn't wait forever, perhaps it was only 42 minutes, but it felt like an exhaustingly long time—which was most likely the point the speaker intended to convey..

When we read the account of the Great Flood, we should think as the Hebrew mind thought. It would be an egregious error to discount or reject Genesis because we calculated the required space within the ark as inadequate to accommodate all species.

The Genesis account tells us that the waters came in such torrents and spigots that even the highest elevations, implying mountain peaks, were submerged. The western mind quickly thinks of Mt. Everest. But Mt. Everest is 29,032 feet in elevation at its peak. That's more than five miles above present sea level.

Mount Everest

Discounting the supernatural, there simply isn't enough water on this planet for the ocean level to be raised high enough to cover the peak of Mt. Everest. That would require the oceans to rise over the entire globe by over five miles from present levels. That just isn't possible. As a consequence, the skeptical western mind, when combined with an internet search for a few Wikipedia facts, has flat out discredited the account in Genesis. While we're at it, this confirms that the entire Bible is just a bunch of ridiculous fabrications.

However, the western-driven mindset is grossly flawed. I am told by reliable authorities that in ancient Hebrew, the word for land (as used in Genesis 6-9 for the flood account) has a wide semantic range. It can mean all the land on earth. It can also mean the land within a localized region. We assume that the boundary between water and air is well-defined. But when a violent overturning would take place, dissolved gases would be released. Vast quantities of foam and froth would obscure the dividing line between water and air. Without a clear definition of the water-to-air boundary, any talk about sea levels becomes obscured. The Biblical account in Genesis is a spiritual story, not a scientific treatise. It is folly to apply science to a spiritual account.

At this point, I will turn to a broader defense of the Bible, and I will use western logic. In the Old Testament, it has been said there are 426 prophecies related to Christ and His coming. Bear in mind that many of these predictions are in the book of Isaiah, which was written approximately 700 years before Christ. The record of Isaiah is rock solid. Historically, we know that book was written. To list just a few prophecies:

- They will hang him on a tree.
- They will cast lots for his garment.

- They will pierce his side.
- He will not break a bone.
- He will be of the house and lineage of David.
- He will be born in Bethlehem, the City of David.

Every prophecy of Christ's first coming was fulfilled. These facts stand as historically attested events.

Consider now if you were to flip a fair coin 426 times. What would you say if somebody could call the coin toss accurately 426 times in a row? Given 50-50 odds of being correct on each coin toss, that would represent one chance in 2^426 times. Two raised to the 426th power is a number so large that it defies any physical interpretation. Next, if we take the inverse of that number, the probability of calling 426 coin tosses consecutively is so small that it again defies imagination. Now imagine that the predictions were placed in an envelope some 700 years earlier, hermetically sealed in a mayonnaise jar, and opened on the Johnny Carson *Tonight Show*. It is beyond any mathematical probability that somebody could predict 426 coin tosses. In a similar sense, no human writers could make 426 predictions and have all of them come true. With that, I say the Bible is the inspired word of God. Only God could have made 426 prophecies and caused their outcomes hundreds of years later.

As a charitable person I will be so gracious as to cut my critics some slack. Even if one would cut the number in half (213 prophecies) or indeed by 90% (43 prophecies), the consideration is still staggering. Nobody short of God can arrange affairs 700 years in advance to accurately call 43 coin tosses. And the Biblical predictions concerning the coming of Christ were much more specific than a mere 50-50 outcome. For example, He will be born in Bethlehem, the City of David.

Bear in mind that the above argument of the 426 predictions was inserted to stay within the western mindset and western logic system. I assert that the observer, and possibly skeptic, has two choices—to either accept the Bible as the living word of God, or to reject it and walk away from God. Again, the evidence in western logic is there and undeniable.

In the account of Genesis, the skeptic is assuming that the oceans are smooth and calm as they rise. Please grant me, for the sake of discussion, my ocean-overturning hypothesis. Any abrupt overturning would necessarily have been accompanied by resultant wave action and dissolved gas discharge. Should ever a deep ocean become unstable and thus overturn, the transient dynamics would be massive and deadly—far deadlier than any event in mankind's memory.

When bottles of carbonated beverages, such as champagne, are opened, it's common for the contents to overflow. We know that ocean bed earthquakes can create tsunami tidal waves.

Wave actions in deep waters involve formidable mechanics. Waves are not linear. The height of a wave, including a Kleinian Wave, will increase significantly as it approaches a shoreline because shallowness intensifies the wave height. As the wave intensifies, a cresting and curling action follows. Waves with curling breakers increase in size.

Even the discussion of wave height is misleading. Wave height is a dynamic property rather than a fixed measure. Large waves approaching a shoreline are deadly. Humans and other breathing creatures are subject to great peril if caught within a large cresting wave. The undertow forces will ensnare any swimmer. Death by drowning is the rule.

A tidal wave several thousand meters high or more, upon striking the mainland of the West Coast in California, would extend inland to wipe out Las Vegas and beyond. An ancient Hebrew author relating this catastrophic event might write, "… and all the land was then covered with water." That coverage can be a sudden and dynamic event rather than a slowly rising but otherwise calm ocean surface. I envision the Great Flood as a violent and overwhelming transient event. The waters rose. Then the waters receded. Genesis does not imply any type of quasi-steady rise in the water level. Any large tidal wave accompanied with torrents of foam bubbles from gases being released would be devastating in its brief but nonetheless deadly effect.

Large Wave with Curling Breakers

As for me, I believe the Bible is God's living and true word. As such, it is fair to ask, just what role did God have in all this climate debate, and what will be the outcome?

I believe that an end time will come. The Bible makes numerous references to the second coming. Jesus will return to Earth and at that time He will gather those who believe to be with Him. Theology and the Bible deal with the supernatural. As humans, we can accept and believe in God, or conversely each of us is free to reject God.

Present-day pseudo-intellectuals declare that the story of the Great Flood is a fraud, claiming that science and western logic are on their side. Yet I've already addressed numerous events in a deluge that would be consistent with both modern science and the Genesis account.

The proponents of science and western logic want it both ways. They claim science disproves the Biblical flood, but they are blind to the 426 Old Testament prophecies.

The point is that mankind has been on this Earth for perhaps 50,000 or 100,000 years. What we might call modern civilization has been around for the most recent 7,000 to possibly 10,000 years, depending on your definition of the start of civilization. Industrialization has been prevalent for a mere 300 years. The Earth's climate rebounded out of the last ice age roughly 12,000 to 14,000 years ago. For virtually all of man's civilized existence on Earth, we have been living in a short little blip, a snapshot in time. But the climate is dynamic, always changing. For human beings to somehow expect that the store will remain open, there will be business as usual, *and they lived happily ever after* is nothing short of indulging in pure fantasy.

Scripture tells us of the coming end times. We don't know the when and the how. It isn't in God's plan for us to know. Certainly, I am not about to get all up in arms over the fear that the sky is falling or that the Earth will turn into a snowball or that the icecap on Antarctica will slide off into the sea. It's pointless for mankind to try to outguess God. Instead, we are to trust in the Lord, and to be faithful to Him.

I would want to examine what feedback theoreticians call the deadbeat response. When a dynamic system oscillates about, hitting it with an abrupt external force can either make the oscillation diminish, or conversely may increase its magnitude. It largely boils down to the timing of the strike with respect to the system's movement. Similarly, burning fossil fuels can either amplify the warming or diminish it. We should analyze the effects—if any—then determine if they bring good or cause harm. My view is that making use of fossil fuels brings good, as it improves the standard of living for mankind.

Special acknowledgement is extended to Vicki Klein Tatko for her helpful insights into the original Hebrew text of Genesis.

APPENDIX C: THIS ISN`T WHY

THE DISCUSSION OF CLIMATE CHANGE and the pending doomsday permeate our culture and society. There is a pronounced tendency for pundits to inject three words: "This is why." As an illustration of the "this is why" mentality, I am reminded of the award-winning book *The Way Things Work* by Macaulay [36]. Macaulay perpetuates an unproven myth concerning the role of bicycle stabilization. To boil down matters, Macaulay asserts that a bicycle functions because of the action of precession.

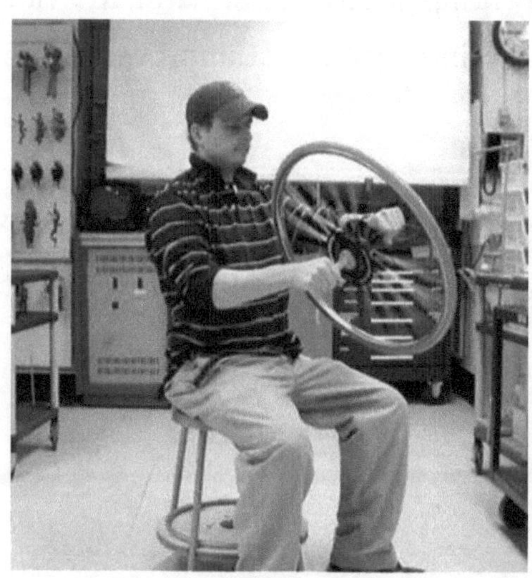

Spinning a Bicycle Wheel

Shown above is the classic demonstration of someone sitting on a stool while holding a spinning bicycle wheel. Spinning the wheel and being twisted about when the axle is inclined isn't the same as actually riding a bike.

What usually occurs during the above demonstration is that the physics instructor or some know-it-all adds the remark, "And this is why a bicycle works."

Macaulay and legions of science teachers make the claim that a bicycle stays upright because of precession, but their statements don't adhere to actual science. With the help of my many students at the University of Illinois in the 1980s, I constructed and tested a bicycle wherein the precession action of the wheels was cancelled.

One of my students, Jadon Evans, riding the zero-gyroscopic bike

For most people the word "precession" doesn't mean anything. Precession is a term from physics that denotes a reaction based on the conservation of angular momentum. The word "gyroscopic" brings to mind the image of a gyroscope. Because of this, I call it a zero-gyroscopic bike, but the correct terminology should instead be a zero-precession bike.

The bike was not only rideable; it was, in fact, easily rideable. The two upper wheels rested on the two lower wheels and counter-rotated, which cancelled the precession effects.

This bike created a stir because many well-informed people had bought into the assertion that the spinning action of the wheel is what makes it possible to ride a bike. The important word in that assertion is "is." As various experiments attested, gyroscopic action (precession) is helpful in bike-riding, but it isn't the one and only thing that allows a bike to be ridden. My experiments with real precession-canceling bikes smashed that assertion to pieces. Physics instructors making such claims had jumped to a conclusion but never tested the hypothesis with an actual bicycle experiment. Once my students and I performed such experiments on real bikes, all arguments were terminated.

One of my favorite expressions is, "Reality doesn't lie." Conduct an experiment and the outcome will always reveal the truth.

Another factor that reinforces the "this is why" reasoning is the failure of many to understand feedback systems dynamics. When a collection of components is assembled and operating simultaneously, the assembly is either stable or unstable based on the dynamics of the whole. In feedback systems terminology, the correct statement regarding stability is "the combined system is stable if and only if all roots of the characteristic equation have negative real parts." In essence, the combined system acts as a single entity and the stability of that entity is determined by the mathematical properties of the whole. Persons who point to one object or thing and say "this is why" are in error. The preferred statement should be "this isn't why."

As we discuss the climate stability issue, it is a similar disservice of science for someone to say "this is why." The stability and thus the behavior of any combined system must be resolved by looking at the whole of the simultaneous actions of the many components.

A Note from the Author

Dear Reader,

Thank you for taking the time to read this book. As an 80-something-year-old retired professor, I finally found time to document my hypothesis on the question of glacial causation. I'm thrilled to be able to share my thoughts with the world and hope this is the beginning of a bigger discussion about climate change. I'm glad you are part of the journey.

If you enjoyed this book, I'd appreciate it if you left a review on Amazon. Reviews help other readers decide to try out a new book. Just a sentence or two saying what you liked about the book will do!

Thanks again for reading and for helping get my books into the hands of other readers.

Blessings,
Richard E. Klein

More Titles from Richard E. Klein

The Deadly Gamble: A Post-Mortem of the World Trade Center Collapse

The Bike Whisperer: Changing the World One Bike Rider at a Time

Dumb Dickie: A Memoir of Learning, Growth, Hope, and Blunders

Kisses When I Get Home: Letters of a Long-Distance Courtship During World War II

Enlightenment & Resolve: Musings from Selected Journal Entries

Dear Valerie: Letters of Wisdom & Philosophy from Father to Daughter

Circling the Drain: Humorous Musings on Becoming a Mechanical Engineer

Second Dissertation Upon Roast Pig: Practicalities and Philosophies for the 21st Century

Bikes Are Big on Planet Klynia (A Children's Book)

We're All Set: Selected Klein Family Memories

Danish Dinner Party: Traditions and Recipes

Denmark to Dakota: The Story of a Danish-American Immigrant Family

About the Author

Birth records state that Richard Klein was born in Stratford, Connecticut, in 1939. This may be true, but he believes, or at least suspects, that he is much older. He considers himself to be a time traveler, a person from the past, a man from the Renaissance. The idea of time travel has a certain appeal, such as in *A Connecticut Yankee in King Arthur's Court* by Mark Twain. By going back 1,300 years, Twain's time traveler had amazing advantages—like knowledge of gun powder and the ability to predict a solar eclipse.

In Richard's case, he has traveled forward in time rather than backwards. His brain is wired as a Renaissance thinker, giving him an enormous edge over today's thinkers. Though many assume we live in an enlightened age of modern science and advanced thinking, Richard strongly argues to the contrary. People today look to high priests and scribes for answers. People fall for myths and falsehoods like this whopper: The Earth will cease being habitable, say, in 12 years.

Because Richard is 400 or so years old, he possesses reasoning skills way ahead of our present dark age cultural norm. As a generalist, he has broad problem-solving skills.

Richard earned his doctorate from Purdue University in 1969 and taught for three decades at the University of Illinois. Richard's research interests are broad, but the main topics he's focused on are stabilization of skyscrapers, teaching children to master bike riding, and explaining glacial causation. Richard is cited in the World

Directory of Mathematicians, 1974. Richard holds Life Memberships in ASME and IEEE, and has been honored over his career with numerous awards, including his paper co-authored with Åström and Lennartsson [17] that won the award for the best IEEE paper in 2005.

Richard has considerable experience regarding heat and how to roast things over a fire. Richard is the 1988 master pork chef of the state of Illinois. Richard has roasted approximately 250 hogs as well as 150 lambs during his years as a gourmet chef. Richard certainly can speak to what happens and doesn't happen when you expose an object, be it the Earth or a pig, to a radiant source.

Richard and his wife Marjorie have two grown children and six grandchildren. In his retirement, Richard devotes much of his time to writing books.

Table of Illustrations

References

1. Klein, Richard E. (2020). *Shivering: Heating Up the Global Warming Debate*, first edition. Dumb Dickie Press.

2. Klein, R. E., V. P. Crome, W. R. Heitschmidt, and C. M. Zinn, "The Greenhouse Effect, Ice Ages, and Atmospheric Carbon Dioxide Revisited via Simulation and Nonlinear Feedback System Theory," *Proceedings of the Summer Simulation Conference*, San Diego, CA, 904-909, June 1972.

3. Dell'Amore, Christine, "Russian Scientists Breach Antarctica's Lake Vostok-Confirmed," *National Geographic News*, 9 February 2012. <https://www.nationalgeographic.com/science/article/120208-russians-lake-vostok-antarctica-drilling-science>

4. EPICA community members. "Eight glacial cycles from an Antarctic ice core." *Nature* 429, 623–628 (2004). <https://doi.org/10.1038/nature02599>

5. EPICA sediment core graph. By Dragons flight (Robert A. Rohde), svg by Jo - svg-version of Five_Myr_Climate_Change.png; original image by User:Dragons flight, based on data from Lisiecki and Raymo (2005), CC BY-SA 3.0, <https://commons.wikimedia.org/w/index.php?curid=5891468>

6. Owen Gaffney, Ninad Bondre, et al, "Interconnected risks and solutions for a planet under pressure", *2012 United Nations Rio+20*

Summit Policy Brief, The International Geosphere-Biosphere Programme.

7. Gear backlash image. en:User:GearHeads, User:Slashme, CC BY-SA 3.0 <https://creativecommons.org/licenses/by-sa/3.0>, via Wikimedia Commons.

8. Prey-predator cycles chart. Image made by K. Menking from data presented in an image in Merritts, Menking, and DeWet, 2014 along with two Wikipedia creative commons photos, available through a Creative Commons Attribution-NonCommercial-ShareAlike license <http://creativecommons.org/licenses/by-nc-sa/3.0/>.

The two Wikipedia images are at:

<http://commons.wikimedia.org/wiki/File:Canadian_lynx_by_Keith _Williams.jpg> and

<http://commons.wikimedia.org/wiki/File:Snowshoe_Hare_(618710 9754).jpg>.

9. Latour, Pierre. *Atmospheric Carbon Dioxide Lags Temperature: The Proof*, 13 June 2014. <https://principia-scientific.org/atmospheric-carbon-dioxide-lags-temperature-the-proof/>

10. *Big Jake*, Batjac Productions, 1971. <https://www.imdb.com/title/tt0066831/characters/nm0000078>

11. Evans, Bill; Kling, George; Kekesi, Alex. "Moving from Lake Monoun to Lake Nyos." *NASA/Goddard Space Flight Center Scientific Visualization Studio*, 10 January 2002. <https://svs.gsfc.nasa.gov/2350>

12. *Energy Sources, Biology for Majors II*, Lumen Learning. <https://courses.lumenlearning.com/wm-biology2/chapter/energy-sources/>

13. "What was the Lake Nyos disaster and why did it happen?" 13

May 2022, *Discovery*.

<https://www.discoveryuk.com/mysteries/what-was-the-lake-nyos-disaster-and-why-did-it-happen/>

14. Schirber, Michael. "Snowball Earth Might Have Been Slushy." *Astrobiology Magazine*, August 2015.

<https://www.giss.nasa.gov/research/features/201508_slushball/>

15. Kaufmann, William J, *Universe, 3rd Edition*, W.H. Freeman, 1991, "Chapter 8. Earth's Albedo" <http://hyperphysics.phy-astr.gsu.edu/hbase/phyopt/albedo.html>

16. Albedo scale. Hannes Grobe, *Alfred Wegener Institute for Polar and Marine Research*, Bremerhaven, Germany, CC BY-SA 2.5 <https://creativecommons.org/licenses/by-sa/2.5>, via Wikimedia Commons.

17. Åström, Karl J., Klein, Richard E., & Lennartsson, Anders (2005). "Bicycle Dynamics and Control." *IEEE Control Systems Magazine*, August 2005. <https://commons.princeton.edu/60-tiger-cub/wp-content/uploads/sites/139/2019/08/Astrom.pdf>

18. Klein, R.E, Cusano, C., & Stukel, J.J. (1972). *Investigation of a Method to Stabilize Wind Induced Oscillations in Large Structures*. <http://pascal-francis.inist.fr/vibad/index.php?action=getRecordDetail&idt=PASCAL7311010028>

19. Maxwell, J. C. (1868). *On Governors*. <https://www.maths.ed.ac.uk/~v1ranick/papers/maxwell1.pdf>

20. Nyquist, H., (1932, January). "Regeneration Theory," *Bell System Technical Journal*.

<https://archive.org/details/bstj11-1-126/page/n5/mode/2up>

21. Kálmán, Rudolf E.. "On the general theory of control systems." *IRE Transactions on Automatic Control* 4 (1959): 110-110. Kálmán, R. (1959).

<https://www.semanticscholar.org/paper/On-the-general-theory-of-control-systems-K%C3%A1lm%C3%A1n/597cf3eb7fbd7c4b231451ec998b8a6ae9996c41>

22. Blumenfeld, R.D., *In the Days of Bicycles and Bustles*, Brewer and Warren Inc., New York, 1930, p. 20.

23. Sergin, V. Ya., and Sergin, S. Ya., (1978) "Systems Analysis of the Problem of Major Fluctuations of Climate and Glaciation of the Earth," *Soviet Geography*, 19:2, pp.99–1360. DOI: 10.1080/00385417.1978.10640214.

24. Ellis, Ralph & Palmer, Michael. "Modulation of ice ages via precession and dust–albedo feedbacks," *Geoscience Frontiers*, Volume 7, Issue 6, November 2016, Pages 891–909. <https://www.sciencedirect.com/science/article/pii/S1674987116300305>

25. C. D. Salthouse and R. Sarpeshkar, "Jump resonance: a feedback viewpoint and adaptive circuit solution for low-power active analog filters," *IEEE Transactions on Circuits and Systems I: Regular Papers*, vol. 53, no. 8, pp. 1712-1725, Aug. 2006, doi: 10.1109/TCSI.2006.879050. <https://ieeexplore.ieee.org/document/1673641>

26. R. Oldenburger and T. Nakada, "Signal stabilization of self-oscillating systems," in *IRE Transactions on Automatic Control*, vol. 6, no. 3, pp. 319–325, September 1961, DOI: 10.1109/TAC.1961.1105218. <https://ieeexplore.ieee.org/abstract/document/1105218>

27. Sergin & Sergin source website. <https://www.tandfonline.com/doi/abs/10.1080/00385417.1990.10

640810>

28. Buis, Alan. "Steamy Relationships: How Atmospheric Water Vapor Amplifies Earth's Greenhouse Effect," *Ask NASA Climate*, 8 February 2022.
<https://climate.nasa.gov/explore/ask-nasa-climate/3143/steamy-relationships-how-atmospheric-water-vapor-amplifies-earths-greenhouse-effect/
#:~:text=Water%20vapor%20is%20Earth's%20most,atmosphere%20trap%20the%20Sun's%20heat>

29. Fogwill, Chris, Hogg, Alan, and Turney, Chris. "Earth's magnetic field broke down 42,000 years ago and caused massive sudden climate change," *The Conversation,* 18 February 2021.
<https://theconversation.com/earths-magnetic-field-broke-down-42-000-years-ago-and-caused-massive-sudden-climate-change-155580>

30. Edwards, Lin. "Evidence of second fast north-south pole flip found," PhysOrg.com, 6 September 2010.
<https://phys.org/news/2010-09-evidence-fast-north-south-pole-flip.html>

31. Buis, Alan (2020). "Milankovitch (Orbital) Cycles and Their Role in Earth's Climate," NASA.
<https://climate.nasa.gov/news/2948/milankovitch-orbital-cycles-and-their-role-in-earths-climate/>

32. Bloom, B.S. (1956) Taxonomy of Educational Objectives, Handbook: The Cognitive Domain. David McKay, New York.

33. Black, H. S. "Stabilized feedback amplifiers," *The Bell System Technical Journal,* Volume: 13, Issue: 1, January 1934.
<https://ieeexplore.ieee.org/document/6767960/>

34. Winston Churchill photo by © Hulton-Deutsch Collection/CORBIS/Corbis via Getty Images.

35. "A Geologic Catastrophe," Montana Natural History Center. <http://www.glaciallakemissoula.org/the-big-picture.html>

36. Macaulay, David, *The Way Things Work*. Clarion Books, updated edition 2 May 2023.